International Relations in a Global Age

For my students and colleagues

International Relations in a Global Age

A Conceptual Challenge

Gillian Youngs

Polity Press

First published in 1999 by Polity Press in association with Blackwell Publishers Ltd

Editorial office:
Polity Press
65 Bridge Street
Cambridge CB2 1UR, UK

Marketing and production:
Blackwell Publishers Ltd
108 Cowley Road
Oxford OX4 1JF, UK

Published in the USA by
Blackwell Publishers Inc.
Commerce Place
350 Main Street
Malden, MA 02148, USA

A CIP catalogue record for this book is available from the British Library.

Library of Congress Cataloging-in-Publication Data

Youngs, Gillian, 1957–
    International relations in a global age : a conceptual challenge /
Gillian Youngs.
        p.   cm.
    Includes bibliographical references and index.
    ISBN 0-7456-1370-5. — ISBN 0-7456-1371-3 (pbk.)
    1. International relations   2. National state.   I. Title.
JZ1308.Y68   1999
320.1'2—dc21   99-12647
                                                                                      CIP

Typeset in 10 on 12pt Palatino
by Ace Filmsetting, Frome, Somerset
Printed in Great Britain by MPG Books, Bodmin, Cornwall

This book is printed on acid-free paper.

Contents

Acknowledgements

As usual there are far too many thanks to include here. Special mention must be made of my family, my former teachers at Sussex University, many of whom have since become valued colleagues and friends, and the British International Studies Association and US-based International Studies Association, where I have found vital intellectual community. Their international political economy sections, BISA gender and international relations working group and ISA feminist theory and gender studies section have come to represent my main intellectual homes and I thank all my associates for making me so welcome and for playing such an important part in nurturing my ideas. Individuals who have offered key support and encouragement include Roger Tooze, Marc Williams, Marysia Zalewski, Jill Steans, Marianne Marchand, Spike Peterson, Anne Sisson Runyan, Jan Jindy Pettman, Hazel Smith, Richard Little, Cynthia Enloe, Kate O'Mara, Cynthia Weber, Rob Walker, Michael Dillon, Michael Shapiro, John Hoffman and Susan Strange.

The approach of this volume is especially indebted to the multi-disciplinary influences I have been fortunate to find in three years lecturing in the Humanities Faculty of The Nottingham Trent University, UK, and more recently in the Centre for Mass Communication Research, Leicester University. The book developed from my PhD completed at TNTU. The staff of the Clifton branch of the TNTU library gave valued assistance, and Hong Kong University library was kind enough to extend its facilities to me for research work undertaken there while I was based at Syracuse University (New York) Hong Kong Center. I am grateful to the following for funding support to attend conferences where ideas were first presented: the Department of International Studies and the European Centre for Co-operation and Awareness at TNTU; University of Minnesota, Minneapolis; the Department of International

Relations and the Belle van Zuylen Institute, University of Amsterdam; the BISA gender and IR working group. I would like to thank all those whose comments on my papers have contributed to the work presented here. My Foucaultian perspectives have been sustained by the History of the Present Group, and the Centre Michel Foucault, Bibliothèque du Saulchoir, Paris, where valuable research work has been conducted.

This book would not have been produced without the initial interest and continued support of David Held at Polity. Special thanks go to him, the Polity team and the anonymous readers whose comments and criticisms proved of much assistance. Throughout the years of this volume's generation and completion, Keith Baldock has been my special companion, sub-editor, and computer and communications ally. His input cannot be easily defined, so I will not try. Warm thanks for everything Keith, especially the positive force of the creative spirit.

Finally, my intellectual debts are vast, and many are clearly noted throughout this volume. The responsibility for what follows rests, of course, entirely with me.

Gillian Youngs
Leicester

Introduction: From International Relations to Global Relations

The basis for this study

The conceptual challenge addressed in this volume relates to dominant state-centric approaches in the discipline of international relations. The central argument put forward is that these approaches have significantly defined the discipline. They have articulated its conceptual parameters in specific and highly rigid terms. The title of the book signals a dissatisfaction with this theoretical deadlock and the desirability of new forms of thinking about what could be more openly termed 'global relations'. The arguments presented trace the basis for this thinking in a wide range of critical work that has attacked the state-centric paradigm from contrasting positions. Thus they contribute to a further development of the critical debate on state-centrism. Their particular quality is twofold. First, they interweave varying critical positions in international relations to identify points of mutual strength across them. The aim here is to consolidate state-centric critique through the identification of these specific connections. Second, they make further links with wider disciplinary debates relevant to such critique. These are mainly in social theory and geography, where the changing nature of the state as a political entity and actor has been the focus of growing investigation.

The context for much of this work has been the phenomenon known as globalization. This can be variously defined, but in broad terms refers to the reshaping of political, economic and cultural boundaries in relation to the expansion of the world capitalist market and its production and consumption patterns, the growth of forms and networks of communications and the widening of political associations and movements (Kofman and Youngs 1996a; Youngs 1997b; Mohammadi 1997; Youngs 1999b). Studies of globalization, for theoretical and policy reasons, have stressed the central importance of fresh thinking about the qualities and potential of states in contemporary times. The influential *World Development Report 1997: The State in a Changing World* (World Bank 1997) focused on the capabilities of states and the possibilities for 'reinvigorating' their institutions. At the close of the twentieth century, the role of the state as key political category is understood to be deeply in need of reassessment on the basis of a 'new geography of power' (Sassen 1996) or a 'diffusion of power' in circumstances where 'the territorial boundaries of states no longer coincide with the extent or limits of political authority over economy and society' (Strange 1996: ix).

The state is being investigated in its global context with focus on 'governance' rather than government, the former breaking down assumptions about national boundaries as sufficient to political definitions of accountability and effects (Held 1995; Hirst 1997). Such debates refocus our attention on how the state has been understood in the past and, in particular, according to this volume, the problem of state-centrism and its conceptual limitations. But they do so in a particular way, emphasizing understanding of the state as political space, its changing relations to economic or market space, and their impact on citizens and citizenship (Sassen 1996). This is the broad context for the discussion that follows. The discussion itself ranges across critical developments and interconnections primarily within, but also beyond, the disciplinary boundaries of international relations to investigate detailed and interrelated ways in which they urge rethinking of the state as concept.

International relations, academically and practically, has been centrally concerned with questions of political control over territorially defined spaces, and the contests, including those of the most violent kind, for that control. The 'power politics' or realist analytical stance (Morgenthau and Thompson 1985) has been viewed as the clearest articulation of that focus within the discipline. Realist frameworks present the predominant tenets of state-centrism: the prime definition of international reality as interactions between states understood as discrete political units (Hollis and Smith 1991: 20–36). The 'reductionism' (Maclean 1981) evident in this understanding of international relations is now a well-established basis of critiques of state-centrism in the discipline.

The major question that this study seeks to address is how state-centrism has *endured* as a dominant paradigm despite such critical onslaught. The use of the term 'paradigm' is important here because it emphasizes a theoretical preoccupation. This concentrates on the characteristics of international theory that define and perpetuate state-centric perspectives. These characteristics, of course, relate to concrete considerations about the changing nature of states and the relative importance of other actors and processes in international relations, but the prime interest in this study is the unravelling of the theoretical problem of state-centrism. As will be explained in more detail in chapter 3, the use of the term 'paradigm' directs attention to the _fundamental_ assumptions underlying state-centrism (Vasquez 1983). The assessment presented here seeks to set out the grounds on which these have endured, including the structure of theoretical debate within the discipline. This structure of debate, which I identify as _superficial paradigmatism_, tends towards the treatment of theoretical developments as separate and distinct rather than interconnected.

State-centrism and beyond

The story of state-centrism's endurance starts with the transformation of realist principles into neorealist ones. Neorealism modified realist state-centric principles to take overt account of the changed international circumstances for US hegemony. This development transformed the realist preoccupation with international politics into a mainstream focus on international political economy. The state/market problematic became central but, as part I explains, the conceptual parameters of the state remain fundamentally realist and the understanding of the market is constrained by these. Structural realism, as neorealism is alternatively named, aims to be a holistic form of analysis: that is, one that addresses the political-economic conditions of international relations. But its state-centrism compromises its potential in this respect from the outset. And, as critical studies of sovereignty have demonstrated, its approach to the state as an acting unit is defined in abstract terms that essentialize state space by framing it purely as bounded territory.

Fundamental to the abstraction too is the removal of women from the picture. Sovereign identity as captured in the state-centric model is inherently male, presenting the state as rational man writ large, a unit that defines political _action_ strictly in terms of the male-centred world of public power – the decision-making spheres of political and economic activity. Feminist critiques of international relations disrupt this abstraction by highlighting the importance of the so-called private world of social reproduction to a deep understanding of _social relations of power_. These critiques are identified as central to the endeavour to de-essentialize state space as it is abstracted through the dominant state-centric paradigm.

The remainder of part I focuses on the state/market problematic in more detail, and in particular on the reductionist approach towards the economic as well as the political sphere evident in state-centrism. Drawing on a range of critical approaches to neorealism and political economy, including those that focus on gender, the discussion assesses the lack of attention to *social dynamics of power* resulting from state-centric abstractions.

Part II locates the possibilities for moving beyond state-centrism significantly in relation to the structure of debate within international relations and its continuing superficial paradigmatism, which emphasizes distinctions rather than connections across different theoretical approaches, and which has been influential in veiling the state-centric bonds between realism and neorealism discussed in part I. The 'territorialising logic' (Ashley 1991) of the discipline has crucially, it is explained, *separated* feminist critique from other forms of critique (Whitworth 1989), a situation that this study seeks actively to address. The whole nature and meaning of theoretical exchange is thus problematized and this has been a major characteristic of the recent 'third debate' (Lapid 1989), providing a focus on theory as discourse (Der Derian and Shapiro 1989; Foucault 1971). This requires an awareness of the degree to which theoretical discourse is embedded in social practices more generally. It is a recognition of theoretical discourse as *a form of practice* rather than as something that is *divorced from practice*. Grounding theory in this way directly addresses questions of time and space. Theory can no longer be abstracted from its social and historical contexts, but must be understood in direct relation to them.

The works of Richard Ashley and Rob Walker, referred to extensively in this study, have been most influential in revealing and interrogating state-centric, sovereign-bound theory as discourse. In international political economy, Craig Murphy and Roger Tooze (1991a) have assessed, from a Gramscian perspective, how such dominant forms of knowledge gain the influential status of assumed 'common sense'. Such critical work seeks to view theory in relation to practice, including in relation to historical and social context. For example, Murphy and Tooze focus on material developments in the post-1945 global economy, the changing nature of US hegemony and the development of theoretical 'orthodoxy'. They support a new 'culture' of heterodoxy, of open critical exchange and 'honest attempts at synthesis', a stance generally characteristic of the third debate. This requires movement beyond superficial paradigmatism.

I argue that feminist forms of analysis in international relations have a particularly powerful contribution to make. They identify gender as a radical category by revealing and investigating in detailed ways the links between theory and other forms of practice that shape social relations of power as gendered. They locate these theory/practice links in a comprehensive sense of social space that takes account of the public/private hierarchies in respect of both subjectivities and actions. It is argued that the third debate, despite its critical richness, has taken power/knowledge issues only so far. It has failed to interrogate its own assumptions about public/private hierarchies, and the pervasive 'territorialising logic' of superficial paradigmatism has fed the blindness to the broad purchase of feminist insights. These offer a complex understanding of social space, incorporating the dynamics of public/private connections, and thus provide an escape from *a gender-neutral sense of spatiality* (Youngs forthcoming).

The rest of part II explores the importance of the normative divide – originally separating idealist and realist approaches to international relations. This oppositional structure has worked in many ways to place ethical or normative concerns *outside* or *beyond* the realist version of politics. The effective result is a narrow and particular version of politics. Drawing in particular on Rob Walker's writings, chapter 4 begins by assessing the ways in which sovereignty as a category in mainstream thought perpetuates this view by incorporating linkages between territory, identity and power. In state-centrism, sovereign political identity is essentially *bounded* identity; divisions between 'inside' and 'outside' are definitive in constructing and maintaining such identity. Sovereignty is a category with timeless, eternal qualities tied to a fixed sense of bounded territory or space. Sovereign identity in this context relates to political subjects as well as states, for the definition of sovereign being is intrinsically collective, dividing polities from one another *and* groups of political subjects from other groups. Such divisions are part and parcel of the *security*, including that of identity, which assertions of sovereign power seek to maintain. Here attention is drawn to Walker's emphasis on the practices of sovereignty, including the theoretical ones encapsulated within the dominant state-centric paradigm.

The discussion then moves to Richard Ashley's (1980) early work on political economy and its investigation of knowledge processes as integral to an understanding of security in international political economy. It is argued that such critiques identify the need to reclaim politics from its state-centric constraints, including those which oppose realism and idealism and thus fail to recognize normative issues as integral to politics rather than beyond them (Frost 1986). The critiques discussed in this volume seek to create quite new analytical contexts for considering normative concerns, opening up the political space that is the state as complex, contested and contingent, irreducible to just the meanings of its *boundedness*.

Spatiality

Part III focuses on the question of spatiality and draws on wider disciplinary concerns, notably in social theory, geography and postcolonial studies. These are becoming increasingly relevant to the discipline of international relations as the state is assessed in direct relation to globalization and globalizing processes. The meanings of state boundaries are problematized in theory as well as in other forms of practice. It is proposed that we think in terms of a political economy of spatiality approach which builds on the critical connections explored in the earlier sections. An examination of the concept of spatiality returns to John Herz's (1957) influential early work on the 'rise and demise of the territorial state' in a nuclear era. This reminds us that, in the key area of security, international relations analysis confronted early on the potential challenge to territorial integrity. Nuclear weapons brought increased state power *and* 'vulnerability'. Herz's work included a broadening of security concerns to include political-economy issues. Neorealism placed these at the centre of its interests, but in the reductionist fashion of state-centrism.

Critical Gramscian approaches have challenged this reductionism and contributed to opening up time/space questions in relation to international political economy. One focus, for example, has been restructuring in the global political economy and its effects on inequalities within and across states (Hettne 1995a). These perspectives maintain a strong purchase on questions of agency because of their interest in counter-hegemonic possibilities as well as hegemonic tendencies. They contribute to awareness that reclaiming the political incorporates reclaiming agency as an active and open consideration rather than as a restricted category in the vein of state-centrism. A radicalized sense of social space is at the heart of gender critiques' attempts to reclaim these areas because of their central concern with public/private social dynamics. Gender critiques open up social dynamics as intrinsic to thinking about local/global relationships; they demonstrate that a sense of the local without such dynamics is partial in the extreme and works on the basis of *assumptions* about the political and economic.

The final chapter focuses on state/market boundaries and the transformative tendencies evident in their interrelationship in contemporary times. The so-called post-cold war scenario that has stimulated so much of the study of globalization features a renewed emphasis on the world economy and its changing spatial characteristics. These include economic polarization between the richest and the poorest both within and between countries (UNDP 1996). Francis Fukuyama's (1992) 'end of history' thesis focuses, in contrast, on a celebratory interpretation of the spread of liberal capitalist values as increasing numbers of people around the globe are integrated into the world economy, albeit on highly differentiated terms. These differentiations relate to consumption as well as production, and direct attention to economic as well as political subjectivity. The growing role of consumption of communications, media-related and various entertainment products encourages thinking about what Scott Lash and John Urry (1994) have termed 'economies of signs and space'. Inequality consequently has to be defined socially and spatially, taking account of the distinctions dividing the information-and-communication rich and poor, and relative capacities to manipulate and transcend time/space restrictions. Such factors come into play whether we are thinking of corporate entities, social groups or individuals, whether of capital, physical or communicative mobility.

The last part of the chapter relates the discussion to feminist purchase on public/private social dynamics and its capacity to reveal the gendered nature of consumption as well as production. Furthermore, it explains the dynamics of globalization as a dynamics of patriarchal forces. A recent collection of essays on Hong Kong (Pearson and Leung 1995b) demonstrates how, for example, gendered forms of capitalist production and consumption meet British colonial and Chinese patriarchal forces. Postcolonial analysis is spatially and temporally sensitive and also addresses multiple inequalities: for example, of race, class or social hierarchy and gender. Subjectivities are key here in respect of understanding agency because they communicate the integrated results of such multiple influences as well as the grounds on which they can generate resistance to and reproduction of established social relations of power.

The parameters of this conceptual journey

It is anticipated that the reader of this volume will have varied interests in its subject matter and an introductory knowledge of the discipline of international relations. However, the aim is to make as accessible as possible the key conceptual points raised about state-centrism and efforts to move beyond it, by drawing on interrelated critical perspectives. Part III, outlining the bases for a political economy of spatiality approach, develops out of the earlier assessments, but ranges more broadly across some writings from social theory and geography as well as from postcolonial studies. The volume as a whole places some detailed theoretical discussion about the restrictions of the state-centric paradigm, and grounds for moving beyond it, in the context of broad considerations about state/market dynamics in an era of globalization.

This is primarily a book about theory, but it seeks to develop an understanding of theory as a form of practice. It seeks to confound assumptions about the separation of theory from practice, about theory as an abstract force discretely fixed in the realm of ideas. The critical work it assesses is in the main centrally concerned with this problem: the need to make the material force of knowledge processes evident, particularly dominant forms that attain the powerful status of 'common sense'. Despite being a predominantly theoretical study, therefore, it consistently makes reference to concrete issues and themes, although these cannot always be developed at great length because of the main preoccupation with theoretical threads. The use of the term 'threads' is helpful in indicating the breadth of the critical discussion and its inherent limitations in exploring each aspect in great detail. It does not pretend to any comprehensive aim of this kind, and to this end provides extensive references for further and background reading. Its concern is to bring out the connections between the different threads and to weave them together as closely as possible.

In breaking down some of the major barriers of superficial paradigmatism, the book sets out why gender critiques and the feminist theoretical perspectives underpinning them are central to the future development of post-state-centric critical thought about global relations. The discussion about feminist work is related predominantly to international relations, but parallels multidisciplinary debates about social relations of power and their gendered characteristics and processes. The spatial sophistication of such analyses is highlighted in this study, which explains ways in which feminist consideration of power across public/ private contexts is deeply relevant to assessments of global relations that aim to expand understanding of local–global linkages. These cannot be negotiated, it is argued, through fixed or assumed notions of state/ market boundaries and their meanings. Critical consideration of this problem is incomplete without incorporating so-called private as well as public social space, and the gendered subjectivities and patterns of production and consumption that define the socially generated distinctions between them.

Part III outlines the conceptual endpoint of this study, framed as a political economy of spatiality approach. The main aim is to illustrate different grounds for linking consideration of political economy and spatiality in conceptualizing global relations. This part intends only to set out what are regarded as relevant bases for further thinking in post-state-centric mode – it provides signposts and discussion about them rather than a detailed framework. Importantly, it locates feminist analysis as central to further work in this area, and explores at length how its approach to theory as practice reveals an explicitly radical spatial content through its multiple public/private concerns. The assessment emphasizes that an understanding of global processes, including those linking colonial and postcolonial patriarchal influences, can often be gained only by precise local study of a particular location and context. Feminist purchase on public/private connections offers the richest conceptual bases for investigations of this kind, which can be sensitive to the interaction of differently located global and local patriarchal forces.

This is a dynamic approach to social relations of power in a complex spatial sense – with an integrated negotiation of both public and private, and global and local. The first two parts of the volume illustrate why such an approach would be considered radical in relation to state-centric traditions and male-centred conceptual constraints. They explain why, even in critical debate, superficial paradigmatism has kept such deep feminist insights to one side.

Feminist thought and the conceptual challenge

This study makes a particular case for the centrality of feminist work in reconceptualizing international relations as global relations in post-state-centric fashion. It builds on a wealth of feminist critique undertaken in international relations, to which extensive reference is made. It identifies this work as part of the collective critical onslaught on state-centrism from contrasting and mutually reinforcing directions. Therefore in many respects it aims to bring feminist perspectives to the heart of critical endeavours in the field, and to emphasize the connections that can be made across it. It offers a fresh conceptual context for thinking through well-established feminist points. Perhaps it could be claimed that it communicates them afresh in so doing.

A number of introductory points should be made in this respect, relating to this study's conceptual orientation. The feminist public/private emphasis referred to throughout is basically conceptual, indicating the need to go beyond the assumed public parameters of state-centric reality to incorporate the private (domestic) world of social reproduction into investigations of social relations of power. There is no intention to essentialize or universalize the notions of public and private; on the contrary, the aim is to problematize them and to recognize their socio-spatial significance.

The term 'gender' is used throughout and this is largely for two reasons. Firstly, in their claims about gender as fundamental to social power, feminist assessments are clearly not only about women, but also about the differentiated and socially structured relations between men and women. Secondly, much feminist critique in international relations has come under the heading of gender. Writing has predominantly focused on the omissions and distortions of male-centred theory, and theoretical and substantive issues around the inequality of women. Recently, masculinity has become a focus too (Zalewski and Parpart 1998). This volume's concerns stress the role of feminist insights into social relations of power in general, and concentrate on their importance in this context to post-state-centric reconceptualizations of international relations.

The use of the term 'patriarchy' in this study demonstrates an interest in the holistic and historic impacts of gender inequalities. By holistic I mean that patriarchal influences are understood to operate across both public and private settings, and are not restricted to family or political structures (Youngs forthcoming). Debates over patriarchy have a long history and 'patriarchal confusions' abound, largely, as Carole Pateman (1988: 20) has argued, because the term 'has yet to be disentangled from patriarchal interpretations of its meaning'. The discussion that follows uses patriarchy in the broad-brush manner outlined above and seeks, if anything, to contribute to the debate about its nature and contrasting forms. It recognizes patriarchal forces within the state as well as the market, and thus incorporates notions of 'social and sexual divisions of labour' (Mies 1986: 38). Its focus is on patriarchal influences in the global context, hence the attention to colonial–postcolonial dynamics. It links patriarchy to investigations of globalization and, in association, global–local considerations to feminist perspectives on spatiality.

Back to the state

The concluding thoughts make clear that it is not this volume's overall intention to suggest that international relations should or will drift away from its preoccupation with the state. The indication is quite the reverse, that the intensity of interest in the state will continue and can even be considered to have deepened in contemporary circumstances. The arguments do claim, however, that there is an urgent need to move beyond both the constraints of the state-centric paradigm in analysis of the state, and embedded assumptions about the meanings and effects of political and economic boundaries. It is argued that the state as a political unit cannot usefully be taken as given, but needs to be more openly explored with a strong sense of how it may be transforming in different contexts as well as maintaining stability. State/market interactions are key to such a complex approach, which locates consideration of the state in a political-economic rather than a purely political context. Abstract notions of the state as a discrete bounded entity, which are embedded in the state-centric paradigm, hinder rather than facilitate conceptual negotiation of such interactions and their impact on shaping and re-shaping the social meanings of boundaries – hence this study's main preoccupation with the unravelling of that paradigm, in part to open up new perspectives on the state.

Part I

Inside State-centrism

This part of the book looks inside state-centrism by examining the state/ market problematic as addressed by neorealism, and by tracing, through various critical lenses, its inherently individualistic, state-driven concept-ualization of international relations, as well as its bases for maintaining a distinct separation of state and market. Drawing in particular on the work of John Maclean, Rob Walker and Richard Ashley, I examine the detailed characteristics of the state-as-actor realist model and its endur-ance in neorealist guise. Specifically, I examine how this model in its realist form collapses effectively the notions of actor and agency, the con-ceptual motif for this process being the state-as-man-writ-large image. Sovereignty and the associated concepts of sovereign actor, sovereign man, are explored as central to the mystique surrounding state-centrism as a dominant mode of thought. The persistence of Thomas Hobbes's notion of the state as artificial man is assessed, as is the role of boundaries in defining this acting entity.

Walker's and Ashley's varied investigations of sovereignty link the sovereign condition, which affirms political identity strictly in inside/ outside terms, to wider conditions of existence in modernity based on power dualisms such as subject/object, man/woman and science/ nature. The other, the oppositional force to sovereignty is anarchy, as Ashley maps in his analysis of 'the anarchy problematique'. He explains how the sovereignty/anarchy relationship is hierarchically defined in terms of presence over absence. Sovereignty as a realist concept is fun-damentally the ultimate expression-of-being in state-centric thinking.

While sovereignty tends to be an implicit rather than an explicit category in neorealist analysis, I assess how neorealism, notably as articulated by the theorist generally accepted as its founder, Kenneth Waltz, continues the conflation of actor and agency developed in realism. Neorealism's major claim to being a structural form of analysis is inescapably compromised by its foundational realist state-centric principles. In realist fashion, the main structural condition recognized is that of anarchy. This identifies structure in a timeless way, not as part of a dynamic historical process. Critiques of neorealism – for example, by Alexander Wendt – have helped us to understand how conceptualization of international relations in anarchic terms obscures agency/structure questions and issues.

Embedded within this position in dominant state-centrism is the gendered conceptualization of the state as rational man writ large. This reflects state-centrism's fundamental qualities as a male-centred representation of patriarchal political practice. Gender critiques, particularly by theorists such as Ann Tickner and V. Spike Peterson, explore the central role in this practice of the public/private divide: the separation of the mainstream world of public influence and work in politics and economics, and the private sphere of social reproduction, family and home. State-centrism, in common with other dominant forms of political and economic theory, prioritizes the presence of the public over the absence of the private and correspondingly the presence of men over women. While state-centrism works to obscure public/private connections, gender critiques seek to expose them and explain why they are fundamental to understandings of deep social relations of power, importantly of political *and* economic character (in state and market).

Chapter 2's examination of the conceptual determinism of state-centrism probes a number of major facets of its reductionism together with its tendency to present a static rather than dynamic interpretation of international relations, including of states as political entities. This chapter fleshes out an important quality of the volume: its distinction between a focus on states and the *particularistic* focus on states offered by state-centrism. The arguments presented emphasize the degree to which state-centrism features narrow conceptual parameters and fails to explore states as historically created and contingent entities, treating them rather as given and uncontested units of analysis. In contrasting ways the critical work discussed illustrates why and how this is the case and demonstrates an active interest in alternative dynamic understandings of states and the discourses associated with them.

The chapter concentrates on the theme of political economy, exploring the critical work of Ashley on neorealism's impoverishment of the realist position through an economistic turn. This identifies the key actors, states, in a supra-rationalistic mechanistic manner, drawing away from an emphasis on politics as the realm of competing interests. This economism tells us as much about neorealism's approach to economics as about its approach to politics. The result is a fusion of politics and economics in a static, deterministic fashion, not the open investigation of the dynamics of political economy in historically sensitive ways. This situation adds further, it is explained, to a precise understanding of the meanings of neorealism's collapse of actor, agency and structure.

I argue that Ashley's critique demonstrates how neorealism *separates* and *relates* politics and economics to produce an effectively apolitical, abstract framework for analysis. John Maclean's Marxist perspective provided early insights into the constraints of neorealist method, particularly its lack of a focus on political economy in the context of the development of social relations. Maclean's critique emphasized neorealism's partialities as a form of knowledge about the world. Other critical approaches to international or global political economy, as it has increasingly been termed, have focused on this theme, it is explained. Notable among these are Gramscian critiques led by Robert Cox, and Susan Strange's four-pronged structural power approach (security, production, finance and knowledge).

Chapter 2 ends with an extensive discussion of gender critiques which have consistently addressed the problem of knowledge and its application, and the impossibility of considering either without taking power into account. I explain how these forms of critique, especially in their focus on public/private dynamics, are deeply disruptive of state-centric assumptions about separations between, for example, political/economic and domestic/international. Cynthia Enloe's attention to public/private connections in that most macho of areas, security, is highlighted as profoundly influential in this respect. It is stressed that gender critiques, in focusing directly on social relations of power and the mutual reinforcements of patriarchal practices across different social spheres, offer a dynamic approach to political economy and thus an important route of escape from the static determinism of state-centrism.

1 | Embedded State-centrism: From Realism to Neorealism

State-centrism has become embedded in the transition of realism to neorealism and the latter's reformulation of the analysis of power as hegemony in international relations. The realist tradition has always emphasized state-to-state relations, interpreting power as the pursuit of state interests and focusing centrally on the politics of diplomacy (Morgenthau and Thompson 1985). It is state-centric to the extent that it *defines* international relations within these strict parameters, as this section and the next will explore in detail. Sovereignty is a key concept here, encapsulating the political identity of states based on their capacities to exercise power and authority internally and externally (Camilleri and Falk 1992: 11–43). Sovereign identity is tied to the bounded territorial nature of states according to realist perspectives. The development of the realist tradition in the discipline of international relations occurred in the context of the breakdown of the interwar peace and the outbreak of World War Two. It marked a transition from the idealist phase (which will be discussed in chapter 4) and drew on founding political theorists of the modern state such as Thomas Hobbes, referred to below.

The development of neorealism reaffirmed the US dominance of the field and its tendency to reflect 'particular aspects of national concern and perception' (Tooze 1984: 5). The neorealist focus on hegemony significantly sought to take more direct account of economic power in relation to state power, notably that of the USA. The growth of neorealist analysis in the USA from the 1970s has been tied directly to concerns about tests of its economic supremacy, as evidenced in the oil crises of that decade and the weakening of the Bretton Woods financial system (Tooze 1987). Hegemonic stability theory (HST) indicated concerns about what challenges to US power might mean for world order, economically as well as politically (Keohane 1989: 74–100). Robert Keohane's

After Hegemony (1984) is a key neorealist statement on 'cooperation and discord in the world political economy'. His fundamental concept in this study is 'interdependence', which has become an influential term in the everyday vocabulary of international relationists (see also Keohane and Nye 1989; Jones and Willetts 1984; Jones 1995). In Keohane's (1984: 6) framework it represents an expansion of the realist perspective's emphasis on competition and striving for power as means and ends (Morgenthau and Thompson 1985) to include the cooperation that results from 'mutual interests'. His main focus is on relations between the advanced industrialized nations on the basis of 'given' interests and existing interdependence. In true realist and neorealist fashion, its preoccupations are with states and with those states with the most power (Waltz 1979).

The development of realism evident in this neorealist framework concerns, as do neorealist approaches more generally, how we might understand that power, the reasons for its existence, its operation and maintenance: in other words, the nature of hegemony. Hegemonic power is multifaceted – military, political and economic. One of neorealism's main developments was a more detailed focus on the linkages between political and economic factors in international relations. Interdependence and the associated notion of 'regime' represent the main conceptual developments of neorealism for these purposes. Regimes are conceived in many different ways (Krasner 1983), but are basically interpreted as representing 'rules, norms, principles, and decisionmaking procedures' (Keohane 1984: 8). So the neorealist conceptual framework considers power as hegemony in the context of interdependence and the role of regimes. As in realist analysis, the intention is to explore the bases for *international order* (p. 9). The crucial question, particularly for Keohane, but also for neorealism in general, is how such order will be maintained after 'the decline of American hegemony' (p. 15; see also Gilpin 1975, 1981, 1987). Keohane's conclusions place great emphasis on 'institutionalism' for easing conflicts caused by interdependence and generating 'cooperation without hegemony' (Keohane 1984: 243–4). In Keohane's assessment, US hegemony left an important 'legacy' of regimes whose effects would endure and which could be regarded as 'a valuable foundation for constructing post-hegemonic patterns of cooperation' (pp. 244–5). Such regimes should be valued for the particular settings they provided for continuing international engagements on the basis, at least to some degree, of shared rules and information.

It is largely because of its stress on regimes and cooperation that 'neoliberal institutionalism' (Baldwin 1993a; Keohane 1993) is now identified as a theoretical development distinct from neorealism (Baldwin

1993b: 9). Robert Keohane is established as the leading proponent of neoliberal institutionalism, and much of the early work undertaken by him on questions of transnationalism, including with Joseph Nye (Keohane and Nye 1972 and 1989 (1977)), predated what has come to be known as the founding theoretical text of neorealism by Kenneth Waltz (1979). I would argue that neoliberal institutionalism contributed directly to the transformation of realism and thus to neorealist developments more broadly. I would further argue that it is more logical to identify neoliberal institutionalism as a distinct variant of neorealism than to identify it as a separate theoretical school. This assessment is based on prioritizing the importance of what they share (Powell 1994) rather than their tensions, as articulated in the 'debate' between them, important as these may be (Baldwin 1993b). Their conceptual roots are realist in state-centric terms. While Keohane (1993: 272) has claimed that it is 'misleading' to label neoliberal institutionalism as neorealism, he has stressed the former's dual borrowings from 'liberalism' and 'realism':

> Consistently with realism – and accounting for the fact that it is frequently denoted as 'neorealist' – institutionalist theory _assumes_ that states are the principal actors in world politics and that they behave on the basis of their conceptions of their own self-interests. Relative capabilities – realism's 'distribution of power' – remain important, and states must rely on themselves to assure themselves gains from cooperation. However, institutionalist theory also emphasizes the role of international institutions in changing conceptions of self-interest. Thus it draws on liberal thinking about the formation of interests. (p. 271, my emphasis)

For this study the shared state-centric principles of neorealism and neoliberal institutionalism as illustrated here are more important than the specific arguments about the logic of cooperation that the latter pursues (Powell 1994: 327). The key cluster of such principles has already been set out above, but to it must be added the realist orientation towards world relations as anarchic – their defining characteristic is that they can be considered subject to no controlling, overarching authority. However, there are contrasting interpretations of anarchy that the neorealist/neoliberal 'debate' explores to some extent (Baldwin 1993b: 14–15), and that were already evident in realist considerations: for example, in Hedley Bull's (1977) influential concept of 'anarchical society'. Bull's application of the notion of society (usually understood in the national sense) to international relations emphasized cooperation through 'common values' and 'common institutions' (p. 13).

The central question remains for neorealists in general, as for realists, how is order maintained in anarchy? Simply put, realism's primary answer is that, through the struggle for power, great power is achieved, and some kind of order is imposed through multipolar or bipolar forms of 'balance of power'. Neorealism's extension of this interpretation represents a development of realism's approach to power, whose more negative Hobbesian aspects seemed less and less appropriate the further we came from the point of distinctively comprehensive US power, politically, economically and militarily, at the end of World War Two (Ambrose 1988: xiii). John Ruggie's (1983) notion of 'embedded liberalism' was powerful in capturing the much-changed situation of the 1970s. In the wake of the disasters of the Vietnam War, the rise of the economic influence of Europe and Japan, oil shocks and the compromising of the dollar's pivotal role in the Bretton Woods system[1] (Kennedy 1989: 533–64), the global reach of US power could be best understood through the values it had championed in the immediate postwar period and their endurance in international institutional arrangements. Such arrangements, from neorealist perspectives, demonstrated the importance of regimes to an understanding of the relationship between power, or hegemony, and international order.[2] These arrangements concerned economic as much as political relations, and were articulated through the frameworks and operations of international institutions as well as through the policies of states.

Keohane and Nye's (1972) early discussions of 'transnational relations' reflected this approach, but also indicated its characteristics as a modified form of the realist state-centric perspective. Their opening statements set out their interest in the degree to which such relations could be judged to have affected state control and operation, and 'the abilities of governments to deal with their environments' (Nye and Keohane 1972: xi). Indeed, their particular focus on the predicament of the USA in this context was explicit, and their main questions included: what are the implications of transnational relations for US foreign policy, and, insofar as the USA is preponderant in transnational activity, what dangers as well as opportunities does this present to American policymakers? Their questions included consideration of how transnational relations tested the established understanding of international organizations. This was clearly a significantly expanded realist orientation.

The continuities and discontinuities across realist and neorealist approaches have yet to be fully explored.[3] While neorealism broadly continued realism's assertion of the primacy of politics (Waltz 1979, 1986; see also Buzan, Jones and Little 1993), many of its forms of analysis, as already suggested, enhanced its attitudes towards power, emphasizing economic power and transnationalism variously interpreted. It is self-evident that neorealism marked a growth of mainstream interest in political economy, but there is much that remains to be said about the meanings related to this move (Tooze 1984: 5–6). One of the key aspects of neorealism's preoccupations in conceptual terms concerns its status as a theory of change produced in times of major change in international relations. This major change was related to the issue of great power or hegemony in international relations, and more directly to the perceived pressures on the USA as hegemon. What would be the result of these pressures for world order? This was a central question of early neorealist projects. And it was not felt that it could be answered solely with regard to politics: that is, primarily to states. Economics – the market – had to be taken into account.

State/market problematic

Robert Gilpin (1987) engaged in one of the most extensive examinations of what he aptly called _The Political Economy of International Relations_ in this vein. His work compared the _Pax Britannica_ of the nineteenth century to a _Pax Americana_ of the twentieth, and he placed his focus on the relationship between politics and economics rather than 'more narrowly conceived security concerns' (Gilpin 1972, 1987: xii). His conceptualization of politics as state, and economics as market, as 'two opposed forms of social organization', basically identifies them as separate, but emphasizes the importance to international relations of their 'mutual interactions' (Gilpin 1987: 4). In a footnote (p. 10) he signals the 'controversy' over 'the historical relationship of state and market', but states his own position clearly with regard to their level of discreteness: 'State and market, whatever their respective origins, have independent existences, have logics of their own, and interact with one another.'

This position is indicative of the limitations of neorealist approaches as theories of change, and, in their analyses of international political economy, as theories of the changing relationship between politics and economics, states and markets. A starting point that allocates a high degree of separation to these categories is inhibited in its awareness and exploration of issues of mutual constitution. It centrally lacks an open interest in that particular dynamic. In order to explore this point, it is necessary to recognize the ontological as well as the methodological implications of the state-centric disposition. Neorealism both perpetuated and transformed realist assumptions that international relations can be interpreted via the state-to-state model and that politics can be considered aligned with the conceptual entity of the state because states are the major (thus definitive) players in the international sphere. It is the nature of these assumptions as an ontological as well as a method-ological disposition that counts. They produce an obsession with the state which takes it too much as a given both as a conceptual tool and as a material entity. This offers a restricted perspective on both interna-tional relations more generally and states themselves in particular.

One of the most powerful recent criticisms of this form of theory is that it has told us all too little about states in practice, outside of the parameters of important areas such as foreign policy analysis, with its prime focus on state-to-state relations. As Rob Walker (1993: 125) stated: 'it would be difficult to argue that theories of international relations possess anything like an adequate account of the nature of the state or the diversity of state formations, or even that they show much concern for questions about the relative autonomy of states from civil society or economic determinations'. This situation is linked directly to the ways in which international theory has tended to take up the tale of the world from the point at which political theory ends (pp. 125–6; see also Maclean 1981). The conceptual standpoint of state-centric international theory has been to look out on the world, to explain it from a basis that assumes the state to be a coherent entity, whose inner workings it is the task of political theory to explore.

It is necessary to understand as fully as possible the characteristics of this analytical position in order to have some detailed awareness of the precise abstraction that state-centrism represents. It is a position that locks us into a kind of ontological no man's land where time and space no longer exist in any significant form, and where boundaries are re-duced to their mere qualities of containment, their definitions of 'inside' and 'outside' (Walker 1993; see also Ashley 1991). This may seem a dram-atic statement, but it serves to highlight the degree of emptiness pro-duced by the conceptual trappings of state-centrism. The state becomes a feeble category, lacking internal substance and defined externally along rigid lines. Simply because realism and neorealism have been able to maintain the hierarchical status of the state-centric standpoint, one should not be deluded into general assumptions about the *power* of their state-as-concept position. The ways in which this abstracts the state in re-lation to the international or the global setting is an undeniable weakness.

This point is demonstrated well by John Maclean's (1984) assessment of interdependence as 'an ideological intervention'. Following on from his earlier arguments about the 'methodological individualism' of real-ism and neorealism (1981), he has stressed the ontological implications of the wide acceptance of interdependence as descriptive of the con-temporary world. What is significant for him is that the concept of inter-dependence represents a *development* of the state-centric worldview, which first and foremost conceptualizes international relations on the basis of separate 'actors (units)' (1984: 131). Thus, interdependence, while purporting to be a category dealing with interconnectedness at the level of the 'whole system', has embedded in it prior assumptions about the inherent separateness of the main _units_ or _actors_. As such, interdependence can be understood as profoundly contradictory, but such contradiction can be explored only through critical examination of international theory's trajectories and developments over time. Interdependence has been a central category in the evolution of neorealist approaches (see, in particular, Keohane and Nye 1989) and is directly related to efforts to integrate economic factors into the realist framework. The concept can certainly be linked to neorealism's attempts to achieve a more holistic form of analysis, even though, as I maintain, any such attempts are constrained within its individualistic state-centric predispositions. What the arguments of Maclean and other critics illustrate in contrasting ways is that investigation of the _development_ or _transition_ of realism into neorealism has much to say about _how_ and _why_ state-centred analysis maintains its conceptual hold.

The claims of neorealism can be understood only with close regard to their realist origins, and it is necessary to be aware that those origins may be veiled by the new formulations presented by neorealism.[4] Thus the multilayered dimensions of state-centrism as they feature in the history of realist and neorealist thinking, their different characteristics and the ways in which they compound and, in some cases, mask one another can be identified. This situation stresses the historical continuities as well as discontinuities in theory. As Michel Foucault (1969) has reminded us, it is important to look for both, and not to be dissuaded from investigating the existence of continuities even though claimed new forms of thinking might at first suggest that such continuities do not exist. Their shape and implications should be considered carefully.

This story of the subtleties of state-centrism's triumph has started to unfold in recent years, but its full significance has yet to be recognized. John Maclean's critique of the concept of interdependence points toward the key transition in the realist/neorealist theoretical move: in broad terms, the transformation of a theory of states to a structural theory. In many senses, realism can be considered unashamedly individualistic. Its direct preoccupations have been states, their interests, their various forms of power, their diplomatic practices. Realism's _realism_ has been understood to be captured in its means/ends approach to power as the driving force in international relations, their _raison d'être_. As most usefully illustrated by Bull's (1977) 'anarchical society' concept, this was never meant to suggest that no cooperative activities existed, just that

these were less *essential* to our understanding than the conflictual influences. Realism has also asserted the primacy of states in defining
international relations, while recognizing, to some extent at least, the
existence of and part played by other actors, political and economic, in
international and national contexts.

Actors, agency and structure

The issue of actors, however, is fundamental to understanding the
logics of both realism and structural realism, as neorealism has been
otherwise helpfully termed (Keohane 1986b). It links directly to neorealism's overt intention to transform realism into a more holistic form
of analysis, to use that description in its most general sense. Kenneth
Waltz (1986) clarified this in his responses to critics of his *Theory of International Politics* (1979), generally regarded as the founding statement of
neorealism. Perhaps the most important aim he reiterated was to: 'Show
how one can distinguish unit-level from structural elements and then
make connections between them' (1986: 322).

As a number of critics have made clear, however, the major problem
was that, starting from a basis of realism, such efforts were severely
constrained. Waltz did produce a structural theory, and as such it pur-
ported to describe the international system, but not without in-built theoretical contradictions, especially in relation to the notion of structure.
Waltz's structures were, in effect, no more than the product of their parts,
the 'units' – that is, states – and furthermore, in realist vein, the parts
that counted most, 'the major powers' (1979: 79–101, 129–93). Critics
have identified the contradictory *individualistic* nature of Waltz's form
of structural analysis and its innate realist assumptions about the
causal primacy in international relations of 'states-as-actors' (Ashley 1984:
240). As Richard Ashley has clearly stated: 'For the neorealist, the
state is *ontologically prior* to the international system. The system's structure is produced by defining states as individual unities and *then* by
noting properties that emerge when several such unities are brought
into mutual reference. For the neorealist, it is impossible to describe
international structures without first fashioning a concept of the state-
as-actor' (p. 240).

State-centric obsessions impose an ontological procedure on conceptualizations of international relations. What realism did overtly at
the individualistic level of state-to-state relations, neorealism has compounded by incorporating similar ontological and methodological forms
of individualism (see also Maclean 1981) into a framework that makes

claims to holism: that is, structuralism.[5] What we are really dealing with in neorealist dispositions is the survival of state-centric assumptions, including the important 'state-as-actor', in an altogether new guise. The varying theoretical circumstances must be considered carefully. In investigating the contradictory nature of neorealist state-centric structural principles, it is essential to explore the issue of 'state-as-actor', to unpack this notion in terms of its application with regard to unit (that is, actor) and action (that is, agency). When this is done, the complexities of the realist/neorealist conceptual relationship start to become clear.

Realism began a conflation of the two aspects – actor and agency – which neorealism has compounded. In realism the identification of the state as the defining category in international relations dealt with issues of actors and agency in one move. The power of this move cannot be divorced from the utilization of the concept and imagery of _man_[6] as rational actor and the ways in which they overtly and less overtly became integrated into the state-as-actor concept. The direct linkages between international theory and political theory are influential here, especially in the use of Hobbesian-type interpretations of competitive and brutal hu_man_[7] nature as descriptive of the essential qualities of anarchic international relations (see, for example, Morgenthau and Thompson 1985). The question of agency was in many senses a given in the context of the state-as-actor concept of realism: states were ontologically captured as man writ large and therefore implicitly endowed, conceptually at least, with the capacities of decision making, and rational, and of course irrational, action (Waltz 1959). The starting point for realist analysis in this respect was the state as a given unit acting in the world, via its representative individuals and bodies, alongside other actors, political and economic, such as international organizations and multinational companies (Bull 1977).

The degree to which the conflation of actor and agency has been facilitated by the realist predisposition to regard the state as man writ large should not be underestimated. It captures much more than one might imagine of the ontological limits of dominant thinking in international relations. It helps in considering further the nature of the concept of 'state-as-actor' (Ashley 1984) and what is implied by ideas of states acting. What matters is that the state is an identifiable entity, thus clearly bounded. In order to act, it has to be considered _sovereign_: that is, possessing the power to act. This sovereignty exists both 'inside' and 'outside' (Walker 1993), but its meaning 'outside' is defined by the anarchic nature of the international environment. The series of concepts, state-as-actor, sovereignty and anarchy, which provide the conceptual architecture for mainstream state-centric thought, affirm the importance of boundaries, but because of the *given* nature of the state they do not explore the full implications of those boundaries for the power that the state possesses inside as well as outside. The state as rational man writ large looks only out on the world, as it were; he is not reflective. The dualisms that maintain his identity are taken for granted and not exposed; thus his unity is assured and his unproblematic, continued and stable existence can be assumed. This is a fair assessment of the ways in which realism and neorealism have shaped mainstream state-centrism. As already indicated, and as will be discussed further in this study, neorealism has significantly embellished the realist conceptual framework with its structuralist claims. Dominant thinking has thus embedded even further state-centred assumptions at the same time as the complexity of the critical onslaught against them has increased.

This onslaught has highlighted the key concept via which agency is understood to be expressed, action to take place, as sovereignty. Sovereignty is an explicit concern in realism, more implicit in neorealism. It is a fundamental means by which the state becomes an abstract category, thus a means by which that abstraction can be explored. Sovereignty has been the ultimate expression-of-being in the dominant state-centric mode of thinking, but it is a concept surrounded by mystique. In some respects this is not surprising. It carries a weight of historical associations from the times of sovereign power as expressed in the divine right of kings and queens to rule. Hobbes's (1968 (1651)) *Leviathan*, arguably the most influential founding text of the realist state-centric tradition, reminds us of the importance of the association with God carried by this idea of divine right, and yet the fact that the concept of sovereignty is imbued with these religious traces is all too often overlooked in the field of political science, where easy and convenient, if misleading, separations of religion and politics (church and state) tend to be maintained.[8]

In developing a critical understanding of the concept of sovereignty, both aspects of its historical associations are important; they both assist a complex explanation of the full weight of its mystique (Gordon 1991: 9). In the modern world of secular state power, sovereignty captures the rationale for governmental being or essence, but it is also impossible to sever realist reverence for it completely from its deeply embedded historical overtones of the unquestioned divine royal right to rule. The fusion of religious and rational mysticism in the concept of sovereignty is dramatically demonstrated in Hobbes's *Leviathan* thesis.[9] In true realist style the state is at the heart of the Hobbesian paradigm, but the precise manner in which the state is conceptualized as 'but an Artificiall Man' (p. 81) is important (Ashley 1989: 309–13). Hobbes's (1968 (1651)) man/state conflation is directly linked to the manner in which his theorizing represents a bridge between the Renaissance and the Enlightenment eras in his pursuit of the merging of philosophy and scientific analysis. His depiction of the state as artificial man can be regarded as one of the most present metaphors in the history of international relations: its anthropomorphic form, represented in _Leviathan_ as a given unified entity not itself requiring analytical dissection, is basically philosophical, but its mystical symbolic power is boosted by its context: a work claiming to seek truth by scientific means (pp. 81, 100–10). Furthermore, in making a series of theoretical leaps, _Leviathan_ assumes that the whole (the state) is no more than the sum of its individual parts (_men_), who, it is claimed, fearful for survival in a competitive and warlike state of nature where irrational passions reign, are guided by reason to achieve peaceful coexistence and protection from external enemies by submission to the sovereign power of the state (pp. 183–274).

Two basic points should be made about Hobbes's overall argument: first, it is circular in the sense that it starts and ends with the state, in the process providing a rationalization for state power; second, with the aid of a series of oppositions that it asserts – for example, irrationality/ rationality, war/peace, individual men/state unity, and fragmented human power/unified state power – it establishes a self-sustaining, self-rationalizing discourse in which the individual pairs of oppositions are reinforced by associations across them: irrationality is inextricably linked with war, individual men and fragmented human power; in contrast, rationality is associated with peace, state unity and unified state power. Having established that the object of the exercise is to pursue truth by scientific means, the internal logic of Hobbes's framework of analysis is well and truly sealed, infused with a might that excludes alternative interpretations of society and of the grounds for state power, and mystified by the cloak of rationality and truth it has woven. In identifying the state as the only rationalizing category in a chaotic world, Hobbes's argument declares it to be the only available ordering principle capable of protecting fragmented human beings from internal and external threat.

What is important in this respect is that states, while being depicted as rational actors, are not perceived as capable of ordering the external world itself, for the Hobbesian perspective declares that the world is created by God, and so places knowledge of the world as a unity in a mystical religious domain (pp. 81–3, 395–408). In terms of human knowledge, according to Hobbes's criteria, the world as a unity must always remain a mystery. An implicit result of this approach for the scientific side of Hobbes's argument is that human beings cannot rationally interpret the world as a whole: in other words that domain remains for them an irrational one, its only possible rationality resting in God. This is perhaps the most striking demonstration of the way in which Hobbes straddled the classical and modern scientific eras of thought and, by merging ideas and approaches from both, gave his analysis a double force: mystical and rational. This force is metaphorically personified in the notion of the state as Leviathan: defined as the rational solution for civilized existence with the mystical force of representing God on earth as 'that *Mortall God*' (p. 227).

Rob Walker and Richard Ashley pick up the critical story of sovereignty in modernity.[10] Their critiques unpack sovereignty's rationale as articulated in state-centric traditions in the discipline of international relations, and get behind the image of *order* as those traditions have conceptualized it. Sovereignty and order bind with anarchy in the conceptual architecture of state-centrism. De-essentializing sovereignty makes it possible to explore more critically what kind of order it is understood to maintain in so-called conditions of anarchy. As sovereignty has been addressed as the *means* by which order is maintained in an anarchic world, it plays the part of central strut in state-centrism's conceptual architecture. Dismantling it is a crucial step towards disrupting the conceptual closure induced by state-centric assumptions. Importantly, it is a step that aids critical awareness not only of founding principles in mainstream international theory, but also of the social locations and attachments of those principles. In other words, while not automatically or smoothly resolving separations of theory and practice, it problematizes them in significant ways. It denies the neat and bounded co-relation between state and sovereignty that state-centric orientations have maintained, and enlarges the debate about sovereignty to broader social and individual dimensions of power and being. This conceptual and analytical move facilitates the interrogation of sovereignty's mystique and the nature of states as political entities.

Ashley (1988b: 228) has argued that the theoretical discourse of 'the anarchy problematique'

> does not stand outside of modern global life, as if at some Archimedean point, and its workings do not involve a language or an interpretive orientation that is alien to the knowledgeable practices at work in modern culture. Rather, my premise is that the self-evidence of this discourse's representations of the anarchy problematique is attributable to its readiness to replicate, without questioning, the interpretive dispositions and practical orientations that are, in fact, at work in modern culture and productive of the modes of subjectivity, objectivity, and conduct prevailing therein. Its representations are powerful because they replicate on the plane

of theory some of the most effective interpretive dispositions and practical orientations by which women and men, statesmen and entrepreneurs go about their business, interpret ambiguous circumstances, impose meaning, discipline and exclude resistant interpretations, and participate in the construction of the conditions, limits, dilemmas, and prevailing ways of knowing and doing that we take to be the familiar truths of global life.

Ashley maps 'the anarchy problematique' onto the rationalist principles of modern discourse (1989), where the oppositional force of the sovereignty/anarchy (_'presence'/'absence'_) dualism is all important. In this context, sovereignty (sovereign being) is the superior 'homogeneous and continuous presence' and anarchy the 'residual external domain' (1988b: 230). Modern rational discourse impels 'the heroic practice' (see also 1991), invoking, in this theoretical articulation, the state as 'pure presence' (1988b: 231). Here we come to a detailed interrogation of the _abstraction_ that state-centrism maintains, for the purity of the state as presence is dependent upon its 'unquestioned' acceptance as sovereign being, and this automatically precludes critique: 'The state, with its associated domestic society as a well-bounded ground, becomes _the_ indispensable ideological principle' (p. 231).

Walker's (1993: 125–40) examination of the specificities of time/space relations conveyed by sovereignty helps to explain how the state becomes an empty category in state-centric forms of analysis. Such relations strike to the heart of the political, he stresses (p. 128). They also strike to the heart of the political silences of state-centrism, which Walker refers to as 'silent ontological claims' (p. 130). Note his view that 'as historical and social constructs, conceptions of space and time cannot be treated as some uniform background noise, as abstract ontological conditions to be acknowledged and then ignored' (pp. 130–1). Thus the 'levels of analysis' framework's distortion of the perspective on social power relations is unacceptable (pp. 131–2). It introduces an alternative 'vertical' hierarchy (individual/state/international) in which the pivotal category of 'demarcation' is the state (p. 134).[11]

Walker's analysis (see also pp. 141–58) offers a sense of the political, or ideological, nature of the state as concept, and its associated expression in sovereignty as a specific encapsulation of _being_ in delimited spatial terms.

> The principle of state sovereignty is less an abstract legal claim than an exceptionally dense political practice. As a response to the problem of proliferating autonomies in a world of dissipating hierarchies, it articulates a specifically modern account of political space, and does so through the resolution of three fundamental contradictions. It resolves, in brief,

the relation between unity and diversity, between the internal and the external and between space and time. (p. 154)

The *eternal* characteristics of state sovereignty are intrinsic to its abstract qualities; it is taken in state-centrism as an enduring given: 'claims about state sovereignty suggest permanence; relatively unchanging territorial space to be occupied by a state characterised by temporal change; or a spatial-cum-institutional container to be filled by the cultural or ethnic aspirations of a people. Governments and regimes may come and go, but sovereign states, these claims suggest, go on for ever' (p. 166).

Neorealism has proceeded to embed and develop this stance further, resulting in the conflation of actor, agency and *structure*. The general debate about agency and structure has traditionally been fairly limited in the discipline of international relations (Wendt 1987; Buzan, Jones and Little 1993). The blame for this state of affairs can legitimately be significantly associated with the combined 'orthodoxy' (Murphy and Tooze 1991a) of realism and neorealism outlined here. The result is a severely restricted approach to the social dynamics of international relations in their fullest and historical senses. The neorealist structural move, which will be considered further in following chapters, has been crucial in this regard. Alexander Wendt (1987: 342) has described well how the neorealist 'definition of system structure is characterized by ontological reductionism'. Such a notion of structure is neither historically grounded nor dynamic: it does not take account of the ways in which structures are constitutive of agents. From neorealist perspectives, structures exist in a world after states, ontologically speaking: that is, structures are not understood as an integrative historical force in the very existence and nature of states.

These statements about neorealism's approach to structure, however, need to be related to the conceptual conditions of realism upon which it is based. These highlight an overarching, universal and timeless structural characteristic of international relations, that of anarchy. The term 'structural' is being used very loosely here to suggest an all-encompassing quality. This anarchic quality provides an eternal back-drop to realist *and* neorealist theorizing, and it complicates how neorealist approaches to structure can be understood. Anarchy is a given condition for neorealism's structuralism (Waltz 1979: 102–28). This condition does offer some form of historical perspective on international relations, but it is intrinsically undynamic and unchanging; anarchy is an eternal category that is understood as, in principle, unalterably applicable. But it is important to recognize the extent to which it incorporates the notion of the relationship between agency and structure in broad terms, for it communicates the key conditions within which action takes place. Conceptualization of international relations in anarchic terms effectively obscures agency/structure questions and issues.[12]

State as rational man writ large

Sovereign identity as captured in the state-centric model is inherently male, as the state-as-rational-man-writ-large image conveys. This aspect of state-centrism's abstract nature has attracted some of the most extensive critique in feminist perspectives on international relations. These have revealed the construct for what it is – a male-centred representation of patriarchal political practice, an image that continues to veil the very existence, let alone the activities and concerns, of women (Peterson 1992a, 1992b; Tickner 1992). This attack, which reflects broader feminist critiques of the patriarchal orientation of mainstream political analysis, addresses the extremities of state-centrism's notion of actor and agency. It reflects that they are underpinned by a partial and distorted perspective on the political realm, one which fails to take account actively of social relations of power in their widest senses.

The 'gender lens' (Peterson and Runyan 1993) has been about putting women back into the picture, identifying how they are relevant to understanding international relations, but it has also been about revealing the _partiality_ of dominant theories such as state-centrism and their direct relevance to understanding power. Gender critiques focus on what can be thought of in this context as deep social relations of power. While dominant state-centric standpoints restrict themselves to the assumed and given world of public power – the decision-making spheres of political and economic activity that are generally male-dominated and patriarchally shaped – gender critiques go well beyond, analytically speaking, to investigate the deeper story of power underpinning and explaining what lies beyond that world of high politics and high economics. The public/private connection is crucial here. The state-centric, rational-man-writ-large world is the public world of influence. It fails to investigate how that world links to the private world of personal, familial and domestic relations, social reproduction and servicing. It fails to investigate the power relations that connect the private and public worlds, the many linkages of low-paid or unpaid predominantly female _work_ of various kinds that is undervalued or unvalued and that does not appear in the statistics, such as gross national product, through which 'public' forms of power are interpreted.

Gender critiques have thus been revealing a _hidden_ realm of power, one that has a long history in feminist analysis. It is that which connects public and private, men and women. It seeks to explain patriarchal power of the public world and the ways in which it differentially defines roles and contributions of men and women in contrasting social and cultural contexts and their relative forms of power across classes or social hierarchies. This volume explores the meanings of such *deep* forms of analysis of power for moving beyond state-centric reductionism. It draws particular attention to the implications of gender critiques for approaches to the categories of actor, agency and structure, which, it is argued, are severely reduced and constrained by embedded state-centrism. Coming chapters demonstrate the importance of gender critiques for expansion of thinking across all three areas.

Putting women into the picture as actors in international relations has inevitable implications for the ways in which agency and structure are conceptualized. All categories of analysis, in taking account of male/female power relations, inevitably negotiate public/private as well as public/public relations. In particular, this study emphasizes that this has spatial implications for conceptualizations and theorizations of international relations. Public/private dynamics represent spatial sensitivities that are far distant from the state-centric reductionist worldview. They also, it will be explained, represent theory/practice sensitivities that are likewise missing from the state-centric reductionist worldview. These spatial and theory/practice sensitivities assert the importance of examining how social relations of power define *the political and the economic*: in particular, how they define, *including through theory as a form of practice*, key entities such as *the state*. The following chapters reflect on the extent to which these qualities are shared with other critiques, but argue that gender critiques open up distinctive possibilities for fresh thinking in such areas.

One of the simplest and most powerful slogans of feminist theory is that the personal is political (Millett 1977; Okin 1991). It has been an intrinsic aspect of feminist theoretical efforts to redefine *the political*, to reclaim it from its patriarchal parameters, to disrupt the powerful public/private divide that has worked to maintain it as a male realm and exclude women from its practices, its benefits and its processes of definition and redefinition (Peterson and Runyan 1993: 17–44; Youngs 1995b). Jan Jindy Pettman's (1996b: x) articulation of 'a feminist international politics' outlines the complexities of 'writing women, gender relations and feminist scholarship into "the international", perceived rather more widely than traditional IR [international relations]. At the same time, it [the book] argues that gender relations never exist apart from other power relations, and so pursues intersections of gender, race, nationality and class in the international.'

The campaign to have gender perspectives taken seriously as _funda-mental_ critiques of international theory has been under way for some time. The institutional import of the feminist theory and gender studies section of the US-based International Studies Association and the more recently formed gender and international relations working group in the British International Studies Association cannot be underestimated. In varying ways this study highlights how gender issues cannot be addressed without regard to the relationship between borders, identity and power. Gender analysis confronts directly the power implications of divisions between man and woman, public and private, and the ways in which associated divisions such as rational and irrational, science and nature, complement and reinforce them (Peterson 1992b). Thus the complex interactions between varied forms of social, individual, institutional, political and economic articulations of power in terms of such binary and oppositional frameworks of meaning, and the perpetuation of historically established relations of power, are brought into view. Theory cannot be abstracted from this situation, for it is an integrated and historically created dimension of those articulations and relations.[13] This is the context for the next chapter's discussion of embedded state-centrism's conceptual determinism. It outlines in detail its reductionist parameters for international relations.

2 | Conceptual Determinism Revealed

What does it mean to *reduce* the essence of international relations to state-centred interpretations? What kind of world is it possible to see from state-centred standpoints; what is obscured or omitted? Richard Ashley's (1984: 239) powerful notion of 'the prism of the state' as 'an ontological principle' in neorealism is an essential aid in this respect. The idea of the 'prism' usefully captures what is a fundamental result of any assumed analytical position, that it inherently presents a partial view, distorted along particular lines. But, as Ashley rightly points out, a major problem is that this partiality is removed from critical consideration because it is embedded in the analytical starting point as, in his words, 'a metaphysical commitment'.

In this context, 'the level-of-analysis' framework set out more than thirty years ago by David Singer (1961) still has much to say about the conceptual traps confronting international relationists. The framework distinguished between the international system level and states level, with Singer emphasizing the need in any particular analysis to clarify which level was being negotiated and for what reasons. His warnings about the dangers of slippage within the context of a study from one level to another, and indeed the use of the term 'level' itself, communicate well the vertical spatial hierarchy that has tended to be implicit in much of mainstream international relations thought. If it is accepted that the predominant conceptual influences in the discipline have been state-centric, and this study aims to demonstrate that this is the case, then a spatial hierarchy defined in terms of states must be taken seriously. If states are taken to be ontologically prior to everything (Ashley 1984: 239–40) then even Singer's (1961: 89) idea of 'systemic level' and 'national or sub-systemic level' is pretty meaningless. His pronouncement that we can choose between them (pp. 90–1) misses the point altogether that assuming they can be regarded as separate in the first place is itself a statement about the nature of the world and its history.[1]

The state as a conceptual 'prism' is abstracted from its historical and relational settings and this profoundly inhibits sensitivity towards international relations as inherently dynamic and socially and relationally produced. Consideration of the state-centric prism as conceptual determinant elaborates the implications of the state-centric trap for understanding of the *state as well as international relations*. As an ontologically abstract category, the state, through the state-centric prism, becomes also a static category. International relations is reduced via the state-centric prism to an individualistically conceived collection of its parts – that is, states – and thus as a collection of static entities. This is the ontological foundation for the concept of anarchy as the ordering principle among these entities, which, according to the dominant state-centric framework, compete on the basis of differentiated power.

This view of anarchy is in itself, of course, an interpretation of the dynamics of international relations. What I am seeking to show here is the extreme limitations, the reductionism, of such an interpretation of *dynamics*. They do not represent a dynamics that demonstrates how states have come to be formed as political entities or even how they may be changing in that guise. They do not open up consideration of states; they rather close it off. This is because of the particular way in which they define the whole – that is, international relations – strictly in terms of the parts, states, and take those parts as fundamentally given and uncontested units of analysis. This conceptual disposition represents the worst of all worlds with regard to any possibility of open exploration either of the changing nature of international relations or of states themselves. Its state-centric ontology represents a circular logic that begins and ends with the state as an empty explanatory category. As Ashley (1984: 238) has argued in his interpretation of neorealism as an impoverishment rather than a development of realism:

> the state is regarded as the stuff of theorists' unexamined assumptions – a matter upon which theorists will consensually agree, and not as a problematic relation whose consensual acceptance needs explanation. The proposition that the state might be *essentially* problematic or contested is excluded from neorealist theory. Indeed, neorealist theory is prepared to acknowledge problems of the state only to the extent that the state itself, within the framework of its own legitimations, might be prepared to recognize problems and mobilize resources toward their solution.

The conceptual hierarchy of state-centrism thus throws little light on the internal dynamics of state power in any broad sense, or on the interaction of those dynamics with the wider dynamics of international relations.

> As a framework for interpretation of international politics, neorealist theory cannot accord recognition to – it cannot even comprehend – those global collectivist concepts that are irreducible to logical combinations of state-bounded relations. In other words, global collectivist concepts – concepts of transnational class relations, say, or the interests of humankind – can be granted an objective status only to the extent that they can be interpreted as *aggregations* of relations and interests having logically and historically prior roots within state-bounded societies. Much as the 'individual' is a prism through which methodological individualists comprehend collectivist concepts as aggregations of individual wants, needs, beliefs, and actions, so also does the neorealist refract all global collectivist concepts through the prism of the state. (p. 239)

'Economism' as reductionism

Ashley's (1983, 1984) discussion of neorealism's 'economism' explains further the precise nature of its reductionism. One of the central problems of the neorealist perspective for Ashley (1984: 279, 228) is that it represents an 'impoverishment' of the realist project 'by reducing political practice to an economic logic'. From this critical perspective, an emphasis on politics at least offers the chance for an understanding of competing interests and investigation of 'the social basis and social limits of *power*' (p. 259). Although realism is inadequate,[2] it does not guarantee the deterministic closure of neorealism's 'essentially technical logic of economic change' (1983: 465). Central to Ashley's position are the particularities of the neorealist attitude towards the state 'as a transhistorical given' (p. 470). Kenneth Waltz's (1979: 89) utilization of 'microeconomic theory' in the development of his structural realism is indicative in this respect.

> International-political systems, like economic markets, are formed by the coaction of self-regarding units. International structures are defined in terms of the primary political units of an era, be they city states, empires, or nations. Structures emerge from the coexistence of states. No state intends to participate in the formation of a structure by which it and others will be constrained. International-political systems, like economic markets, are individualist in origin, spontaneously generated, and unintended. (p. 91)

According to Waltz, in such circumstances, where survival is the bottom line, behaviour is influenced by identified 'patterns' of success and failure (p. 92).

Ashley's (1983: 483) concerns are concentrated on the neorealist treatment of 'the logic of economy as a surface framework – the objectively given form of rationality – within which the actors more or less consciously orient their choices'. Thus neorealism, Ashley stresses, excludes the critical and 'adaptive' possibilities of politics, and in so doing outlaws the questioning of 'the given order of domination' and 'theoretical recognition' to those forces that might threaten to disrupt its logic, such as 'transnational class interests'. Recalling his early critical work on international political economy and 'processes of growth' (1980), his emphasis rests on neorealism's 'ideological' status (1984: 279) in this context, its denial of a politics that could critically address 'the dynamics of differential growth that contribute to international competition, rivalry, tension, and violence' (1983: 484).[3]

In highlighting the 'economistic' rationale of neorealism's premises, Ashley reveals the nature of the internal parameters that it places on conceptualization. The fact that these are internal, that they are embedded in the foundations of this form of theorizing, is crucial, for it signifies their importance ontologically as well as methodologically. It demonstrates the bases from which understanding of the world commences. Ashley's discussion of 'economism' has emphasized its removal of the _critical power_ of politics. For Ashley, politics provides at least the potential for critical exchange and reflection, whereas 'economism' is deterministic (1983: 464). Politics is a realm in which possible changes can be identified and fought for, whereas 'economism' excludes such dynamic perspectives. Politics can be sensitive to time and place, to historical circumstances and contingencies, whereas 'economism' denies such sensitivity in its abstract and ahistorical tendencies. Politics can be expansive and open, whereas 'economism' is reductive and closed. While 'economism' narrows understanding of human motivation and history along rationalistic lines, politics provides the potential for a fuller understanding of such motivation and history, allowing for radical critique.

The ontological implications of 'economism' are profound. The world-view it permits is highly delineated and reliant on a manipulation of the relationship between politics and economics. Kenneth Waltz's (1979) founding neorealist arguments claim to be a _Theory of International Politics_. The implication of Ashley's detailed interrogation of neorealism's 'economism' is that it has produced a _transformed_ notion of politics. This is quite a different notion of politics from that which Ashley would promote and explore as indicated above. The transformation is central to the nature of, and relationship between, agency and structure, as these are articulated in neorealist principles. Understanding of it develops awareness of neorealism's specific form of agency/structure conflation and its impact on conceptualization of human history and motivation. It is vital in this regard to pay close attention to the particularities of theoretical dispositions towards politics and economics.

The distinctions between neorealist politics and the kind of politics envisaged by Ashley have already been signalled. His concerns with neorealism's 'economism' must also be considered further in this vein. It is neorealism's *particular* purchase on rationalistic, economistic principles as the driving force in political action that requires examination. The ontological bases of these principles tell as much about neorealism's reduction of economics as about its reduction of politics. Perhaps most significantly, these bases demonstrate the degree to which neorealism's foundations actively close off consideration of the nature of politics and economics as dynamic aspects of human history.

This study explores how the changing nature of politics and economics and their interrelationships are fundamental to considerations of global relations. It is therefore important to investigate precisely how neorealism as a dominant theory has countered the identification and examination of such issues. It is especially important to understand how it has done so in a mode that works to reinforce the conceptual closure it imposes on *both* politics and economics. What results is the fusion of politics and economics in a static and deterministic fashion, not the open investigation of the dynamics of political economy in historically oriented and contingent senses. I would argue that, in this respect, we end up with the worst of all conceptual worlds in the neorealist standpoint – reductive *and* static notions of politics and economics. The possibilities for open investigation of politics and economics in relation to questions of time and space are inhibited to an extreme degree. This is ensured by the circularity of neorealism's conflation of agency and structure, which results in the conceptual trap of an eternal anarchic *present* with no apparent potential for escape from its deterministic principles of survival.

An effective notion of agency has built into it issues of historical specificity and contingency; it allows for the investigation of power relations with regard to questions of time and space. Neorealism's collapsing of agency into state-as-actor denies such issues and the richness of conceptualization and analysis they offer. Neorealism's further collapsing of state-as-actor into structure compounds the problem and effectively eradicates the potential for any truly dynamic assessment of structure and agency. It is not an overstatement to argue that neorealist principles work to present a freeze-framed anarchic perspective on global relations for which they make eternal claims. This is demonstrated in the following statement by Kenneth Waltz (1979: 94):

So long as the major states are the major actors, the structure of international politics is defined in terms of them. That theoretical statement is of course borne out in practice. States set the scene in which they, along with nonstate actors, stage their dramas or carry on their humdrum affairs. Though they may choose to interfere little in the affairs of nonstate actors for long periods of time, states nevertheless set the terms of the intercourse, whether by passively permitting informal rules to develop or by actively intervening to change rules that no longer suit them. When the crunch comes, states remake the rules by which other actors operate.

The discussion undertaken in this chapter is intended to illustrate that breaking out of the conceptual trap of an eternal anarchic present concerns the understanding of both politics and economics and the relationship between them. It is essentially a matter of critical engagement with questions of political economy. Neorealist analysis has made important claims to assessment of international political economy, but these claims must be understood in the context of the ontological and methodological foundations addressed in this study. Neorealist state-centrism assumes far too much about states and pays too little attention to the nature of economics in any open sense. It intrinsically maintains the state/market oppositional framework by asserting the hierarchical importance of state over market, and thus politics over economics. Its 'economism', far from opening up debate about economics, embeds a particular form of economistic rationality _within_ its definition of politics, thus also reducing the notion of politics to one in which questions of agency are effaced by eternal deterministic principles.[4]

Fundamental to Ashley's critique are the precise ways in which neorealism _separates_ and _relates_ politics and economics. Ashley's conclusion is that, despite neorealism's claims to an advanced form of theorizing international politics, it is, in important senses, apolitical; it abstracts and economizes the motivations of states as actors, diverting attention from an understanding of politics as a realm of practical, historically located and contingent struggle over competing interests, which may include critiques of the so-called rationalities of the dominant order. But Ashley goes further in relating the neorealist theoretical move to the changing role of the state in contemporary global political economy. Implicit in this approach is a sensitivity to historical conditions that may affect how politics and economics might be defined, or might be understood to be operating. Ashley (1983: 488) points to the importance of 'the utterly transparent and unconcealed economic role of the advanced capitalist state'. The degree to which the state's legitimacy depends on this role continues to grow, he explains: 'The state's performance as rational economic dysfunction manager is perhaps its premier justification' (p. 488).

The theme of the changing nature of the state's role in political-economy terms has been developing in recent years, particularly in relation to globalization (see, for example, Gill 1994; Cerny 1995; Runyan 1996), and this will be considered further. What is distinctive about Ashley's critique is its potential for opening up a whole series of questions within the discipline about 'statism' (1984: 238–42) as a form of theoretical practice. One does not have to adopt Ashley's precise standpoint or be in agreement with his final conclusions to benefit from the critical space that his analysis reveals. It facilitates a de-essentializing of conceptual approaches to both politics and economics in theory *and* practice in the study of international relations. It prompts exploration of how political and economic assumptions and implications may be integrated into dominant forms of theorizing, and how such forms link with other historical developments. It signals that ontological questions concerning 'statism' cannot be reduced to politics, but should incorporate economics and address any explicit or implicit interrelationships between them. Ashley's critique demonstrates that profound questions remain to be asked about how politics and economics are regarded in international relations, and thus about the nature of political economy as it is generally understood. His work suggests that those practising in the discipline may be assuming far more about politics and economics than they realize.

Social dynamics obscured

The state-centric prism offers no penetrating perspective on the dynamics of internal social contradictions or tensions, either within or beyond individual states. This has been a key theme of John Maclean's critique of state-centric ontology from an explicitly Marxist theoretical perspective. Like Ashley, Maclean has concentrated on the assumptions embedded in individualistic approaches, and the implications of his arguments are that these lead to superficial rather than penetrating investigations of the 'contradictory' nature of 'global relations'.

> For example, there is a contradiction between the concepts of a liberal view of international society, that imply freedom and equality, and the true content of these categories under liberal hegemony in which inequalities between people are determined by social and political power. This is not then a logical contradiction that can be corrected in thought, but a structured condition of global social relations themselves. (1981: 112)

Maclean's arguments clarify how problematic it is to regard abstract state-centrism as addressing issues of power and social relations on an international or global level at all. Maclean's assessment, and Ashley's (1984: 239), is that this state-centrism actually works to exclude such forms of global analysis.

Maclean's (1988) Marxist critique of mainstream international relations' inadequacies with regard to political economy conveys a similar message. He explains that a Marxist approach to political economy is 'not only about politics and economics considered phenomenally, but about the development generally of social relations' (p. 300). Affirming that his interest here is in Marx's '_method_', not his '_theory_ of capital', Maclean's analysis clearly indicates how significantly our ('epistemological') basis for gaining knowledge about the world, and our chosen ('methodological') means for doing so influence precisely how we understand categories such as politics and economics and, in their relation to one another, political economy. In outlining Marx's preoccupation with 'the kinds of dualism that sharply separated consciousness from reality' (p. 302), Maclean makes explicit the unacceptability of the 'empiricist', or what he has called elsewhere 'empirico-analytical' (1981: 110), traditions in mainstream international relations thinking.[5] From a Marxist perspective these collapsed the 'empirical' and the 'real', and denied unobservable phenomena 'ontological status as causal mechanisms' (1988: 300). Such points direct attention to Marxist holistic methodology as opposed to the 'methodological individualism' (1981) of realism and neorealism.

> Marx saw analysis as being the attempt to expose the structural conditions for various forms of conscious individual or group action: what economic processes, for example, must take place for shopping to be possible? In Marx's terms the conception of the relation between people, groups, institutions, and society, is that people, via their conscious human activity, for the most part unconsciously, reproduce the structures that govern their substantial and observable activities of production. People do not work in order to reproduce the capitalist economy, but it is, nevertheless, the unintended consequence of, as it is also the necessary condition for, that particular activity. (1988: 304)

The details of Ashley's and Maclean's critiques in different ways point to the ontological blindness that state-centrism and its assumptions have engendered and maintain with regard to global relations. Far from assisting identification and understanding of the workings of those relations, and the nature and effects of power struggles, they obscure them via the state-centric 'prism'. The resultant impression is that the state-centric story of international relations is highly partial and severely limited, and that the story of global relations would otherwise read quite differently, ontologically, epistemologically and methodologically.[6]

Gramscian approaches to international political economy, which represent developments of critical Marxist traditions, have expanded debate on these areas significantly, as this study will explore further. Robert Cox's (1981) seminal article 'Social forces, states and world orders: beyond international relations theory' sets the Gramscian framework in this respect. This article remains one of fullest critical statements of the need to integrate theory into critical considerations of history. Its interrogation of state-centrism's conceptual determinism is overt.

> There has been little attempt within the bounds of international relations theory to consider the state/society complex as the basic entity of international relations. As a consequence, the prospect that there exist a plurality of forms of state, expressing different configurations of state/society complexes, remains very largely unexplored, at least in connection with the study of international relations. (p. 127)

The article's major points include the distinction between 'problem-solving theory' and 'critical theory'. The former, characteristic of dominant state-centrism, takes the world as it is, as given, while the latter 'stands apart from the prevailing order of the world and asks how that order came about'.

> Critical theory is theory of history in the sense of being concerned not just with the past but with a continuing process of historical change. Problem-solving theory is non-historical or ahistorical, since it, in effect, posits a continuing present (the permanence of the institutions and power relations which constitute its parameters). . . . Moreover, the assumption of fixity is not merely a convenience of method, but also an ideological bias. . . . Indeed, the purpose served by problem-solving theory is conservative, since it aims to solve the problems arising in various parts of the complex whole in order to smooth the functioning of the whole. (p. 129)

The Gramscian mode of thought articulated by Cox thus emphasizes the importance of history in relation to theory and practice, with 'the framework for action' being understood as historically contingent and represented by 'an historical structure, a particular combination of thought patterns, material conditions and human institutions which has a certain coherence among its elements' (p. 135). This approach broadens the critical boundaries of the onslaught against realist/neorealist state-centrism significantly. The concern with the realm of ideas as social force has helped to expand the possibilities for thinking through theory/ practice connections more deeply in the context of political economy. For example, from Cox's perspective, neorealism has 'virtually ignored the production process' (p. 135; see also Cox 1987).

Susan Strange's (1994b) identification of four structures – security, production, financial, knowledge – as central to the understanding of the global political economy does not fit into any individual theoretical category, but has remained, since it was first published in 1988, one of the best known and understood structural approaches.[7] Strange's distinction between 'relational power' and 'structural power', in ways which have some empathy with Gramscian perspectives, locates structural power in the capacity to shape the environment within which all operate, and the rules and conventions by which they do so (pp. 24–5). Similar to Gramscian approaches, there is overt sensitivity to history. Even in terms of US hegemony, Strange's explanation of structural power has nuances that neorealist state-centrism could never have. In focusing, for example, on knowledge, including technological capacities and the importance of long-term research and development leads, her analysis develops understanding of specific aspects of US state and corporate power.

In her recent work on 'the diffusion of power in the world economy' Strange (1996: 185) has concluded that her original thesis on structural power in _States and Markets_ (1994b) did not go far enough in examining authority beyond state-centric boundaries. Her explanatory footnote is interesting in the context of this volume's preoccupations.

> as a number of students and other readers have pointed out, there were internal contradictions in that book [_States and Markets_] reflected in the title. While implicitly criticising the state-centrism of most of the IPE [international political economy] literature, I too fell into the trap of concentrating – perhaps not exclusively but certainly over-much – on the authority of states over markets.

She admits that this was 'an error', which broadening her approach to authority, power and politics was designed to correct. She identifies 'technology, markets and politics' as the key focus for understanding change in the global economy, with the last including 'much more than governments and politicians'.

> These are important because choices in technology and change in markets can be affected by the decisions and non-decisions of governments. But politics also includes the actions and decisions of all those who seek the support of other wills to gain their objectives. Not least it must include the actions and decisions taken by corporate strategists as they respond to change in the market and change in technologies affecting the fortunes and life-chances of the firm and its prospects for survival against

competition. Their political decisions will shape the course and development of production of goods and services and thus of international trade and transnational investment. The wealth and ultimately the power, and the relative vulnerability, of states will be affected. (pp. 185–6)

Strange's latest work is therefore delving much further into expanded and blurred notions of politics and economics and political-economic actors, hence problematizing state/politics, market/economics boundaries. She is pressing further her concerns with the impossibility of negotiating change in state-centred terms and the need instead to search for the ways in which state/market interactions shape it. The arguments in this volume clearly agree with Strange's position that the market is taken too much for granted in dominant state-centric frameworks, but go further in problematizing understanding of the political and the economic, and importantly power, in prioritizing the distinctive challenges that gender analysis presents in this regard.

Gender and political economy

The extremities of state-centrism's partial perspectives are demonstrated most dramatically by gender critiques. These reflect on the detail of the static and abstracted picture presented of an anarchic world of states as rational men/actors writ large, and prompt awareness of the importance of gender relations for a deep understanding of the dynamics of global relations. The implications of the points made in the previous chapter are that if mainstream state-centric theorizing has conceptualized a world without women, or, more precisely perhaps, one in which their presence need not be taken actively into account, then it has created and perpetuated a worldview that is as partially informed about social dynamics as it is limited in analytical potential; for gender issues are fundamental to those dynamics, to the *definition* and *process* of power relations. It is impossible to understand those relations, past, present and future, without regard to such issues. And the possibility of understanding them at all is highly dependent on the conceptual categories being applied.

Gender critiques thus address the problem of knowledge and its application, and the impossibility of considering either without taking power into account. They undermine the ontological assumptions of state-centrism and challenge dominant conceptualizations in international relations on their own terms. These articulate the prime importance of power, of investigating power on a global scale, but gender critiques make explicit the limitations of what is meant by 'power', and the partiality of international relations' dominant perspectives on power. In social relations, gender is one of the main means of examining power, of exploring how _public_ and _private_ domains are defined and maintained, of assessing what is regarded as political or economic in and across such contexts.

Gender critiques help us to understand what lies behind the veil of abstraction supported by state-centrism. They demonstrate the influential social processes obscured by this veil and, in their efforts to tear it down, effectively disrupt state-centric claims that the state is unified and coherent. These critiques break though the mystique of coherence in their application of a critical category, gender, which cuts across the divides of public/private, political/economic, domestic/international, in the examination of power. The rational-man-writ-large mode of understanding global relations that is characteristic of state-centrism denies the centrality of gender and thus leaves such challenges conveniently to one side. This is unacceptable not only to those interested in gender, but to anyone concerned with improved understandings of global power relations.

This is amply illustrated by V. Spike Peterson and Anne Sisson Runyan's (1993: 79–112) recent discussion of the linkages between 'gendered divisions of violence, labor, and resources'. It powerfully upsets the state-centric mode, making explicit the global impact of rational-man-writ-large principles, including with regard to environmental issues. The gendered characteristics of western ideology, it is claimed, help to rationalize the abuse of nature.

> Western gender ideology construes nature as a passive resource to be controlled, used, and even abused. As this ideology has become increasingly widespread, environmental crises have followed, ranging from the problems of acid rain and global dumping to ozone depletion and global warming.
>
> Gender ideology is by no means the sole cause of these problems, but if we look through the lens of the gendered division of resources, we see that gender ideology contributes to the growth and perpetuation of these problems. Although there are still cultures that retain some reverence for the feminine principle of nature, the increasingly global aspects of the gendered division of resources rest upon the following dualisms: culture–nature, active–passive, subject–object, users–resources, advanced–primitive, and exploitation–stewardship. These dualisms are manifested in the contemporary situation, where women have a great deal of responsibility for caring for the environment but little say in how it will be used and for what purposes. (p. 106)

The general critical lessons that can be drawn from this form of approach to global relations will be expanded upon further in this study. At this point I would stress their pervasive disruptive force with respect to state-centrism. Their emphasis on the question of social hierarchies and global relations, and their disruption of state/international divides that drive state-centric approaches, are particularly relevant to broader disciplinary debates about globalization. They implicitly as well as explicitly address and enlarge understanding of boundaries, in their full social senses, and their role in power relations. They draw issues of identity into the centre of their considerations about theory and practice, for if gendered knowledge practices play such a crucial part in global power relations, then their linkages of individual, social and global categorizations are worthy of deep investigation. These considerations directly concern social dynamics: 'The content of what the relations of gender look like is arrived at not in any static way but through the activities of real, living human beings operating within real historical circumstances' (Whitworth 1994b: 121).

Gender critiques investigate these dynamic circumstances, effectively challenging the tyranny of abstraction maintained by dominant forms of state-centrism. These critical endeavours to break open the state-centric prism offer a deep route to the analysis of social relations of power, particularly with regard to considerations of public and private. Broadly speaking, in mainstream political and economic theory, these categories are usually taken to refer to general or generalized interests and particular or particularized interests as represented by 'goods or assets', with the most familiar provider of public goods traditionally being the state, but with ideas of international public goods increasingly prominent owing to the roles and activities of institutions such as the International Monetary Fund and World Bank.[8] The whole notion of public goods is problematic in power terms if taken as given because there is a failure to probe the processes and means by which these goods have been denoted as being in the general interest or to the general good. In power terms, gender critiques are more usually pursuing a deeper analysis of public and private, which aids understanding of how interests come to be identified and mobilized. Their emphasis is on what can be captured as the divisions between public and private realms or spheres of activity. Gender critiques reveal the extent to which the definition, operation and manipulation of these so-called public and private spheres are fundamental to understanding power relations (Youngs 1995a).

V. Spike Peterson and Anne Sisson Runyan's (1993) examination of *Global Gender Issues* has clearly set out the extent to which we need to consider such hierarchical divisions across every aspect of personal, economic and political experience and activity. In fact, it is the very mutual reinforcement of such divisions across different areas that is so important. Being considered in this regard are multiplicities of hierarchical separations of private and public that serve to support one another. The understanding of private and public that must be brought to bear here is one in which the private world is subservient to the public: the private as the sphere of domesticity, social reproduction and personal relationships, and the public as the realm of traditionally understood political and economic activities, decision making and war. Where women's influence is concentrated in the private, men dominate the public. Socialized gendered identities follow these dominant patterns, women being identified in terms that link to the private sphere, as opposed to men, whose identities are related to the public sphere.

Cynthia Enloe's (1990, 1993) analysis is notable among many things for its disruption of the public/private divide in that most macho of areas, security. Her writing helps to reveal how the mystique surrounding such an apparent divide is intrinsic to the processes that support and maintain power imbalances across it. In her recent reflections on the so-called post-cold war world, she explains that the 'militarism' of the cold war was not 'natural' or 'monolithic'.

> The militarism that was legitimated when mutual superpower hostilities were at their fiercest had to be fed by enormous infusions of public funds, distorting whole economies in both large countries and small. But even then, militarism couldn't live on money and weaponry alone. It depended upon policies to ensure certain sorts of sexual relations: male bonding that stopped short of sexuality; men's sexual liaisons with foreign women that stopped short of the affection that might reduce militarized racism; misogyny that stopped short of a domestic violence that might undermine discipline and morale; wives' and lovers' sexual fidelity that stopped short of their having any sense of entitlement. (1993: 253)

Peterson and Runyan (1993) have examined at length issues relating to 'the social construction of gender and gender hierarchy', and it is necessary to recognize the ways in which this kind of analysis introduces a sense of history different from that promoted by abstract state-centrism, its eternal category of anarchy, and the high politics orientation towards major events of conflict and cooperation. The world stage of gender analysis features very different kinds of acts, processes and participants from the world stage of realist and neorealist state-centrism, and more complete notions of the ways in which they interact, including through processes of socialization in public and private circumstances. It is quite legitimate to argue that gender analysis presents a much deeper investigation of power relations in this respect.

Whereas the state-centric stage is set with patriarchal structures and influences intact, as given, gender analysis seeks to expose why and how those structures and influences exist. Gender critiques break apart the seamless coherence of the patriarchal picture of global relations as viewed through the state-centric prism and reveal the historical conditions that have produced it and work to maintain it. While traditional state-centric perspectives present global relations as if gender does not matter, gender analysis makes clear how pervasively and essentially it does. This study will explore this point in more detail. At this stage it is helpful to emphasize that public/private connections are fundamental to claims for the importance of taking gender seriously and that these relate to the study of political economy as much as politics. It is essential to recognize that gender analysis has problematized understanding of politics and economics, their categorization and interaction, at the deepest levels. Thus these types of critique offer distinctive challenges to thinking about political economy and possibly the strongest, although as yet not fully recognized, challenge to state-centrism's conceptual determinism in this regard.

This chapter and the previous one have outlined key characteristics of state-centrism's abstractions in relation to political economy, which, it has been argued, lead to a static rather than a dynamic approach to politics and economics or state and market as they are generally conceived, and, indeed, their interrelationships. Gender critiques, in their implicit as well as explicit examination of patriarchal forms of power, offer, on the other hand, a quite contrary and distinctly integrated approach to political economy. They focus on the similarities, mutual characteristics and reinforcements of such forms of power, their articulations and operations, across political and economic spheres.

Richard Ashley's notion of the 'prism' is useful for interrogating the patriarchal worldview of political economy (Youngs forthcoming). The patriarchal prism through which political economy has traditionally been interpreted is based on a prioritization of public sphere activities over the private realm on the basis of a power relationship between the two. The public sphere of states and markets is defined primarily in terms of their major players: governments and transnational corporations as well as the influential international entities involving and/or affecting both, such as the European Union. The statistics that are utilized to describe the power and division of wealth across the world economy reflect this framing of it in terms of these major players, but they also reflect associated narrowly defined interpretations of production and consumption at state and market levels. These are related to the elevation of the public over the private as determinant of international reality, a process that in theory and practice works to obscure various aspects of social reproduction in the private realm: that is, the home and the family (Peterson 1992b; Whitworth 1994b).

So much is hidden from analytical view by the patriarchal prism, which overtly neglects the public/private linkages supporting dominant institutionalized forms of knowledge and practice that define political economy. To interpret the state-centric prism as patriarchal prism is to place critical emphasis on these linkages and their relevance to the re-thinking of agency and structure.

Conclusion

This chapter and the previous one have covered a range of critical work that has revealed dominant state-centrism's reductionist perspectives. The broad implication of the arguments set out, summarized simply, is that neorealism is caught in its own foundational state-centric trap. Starting from realist assumptions, it has no chance of achieving the structural form of analysis to which it aspires, except in a highly delineated, even contradictory, fashion. Neorealism can be regarded as a development of realist state-centrism, but it does not fundamentally alter its worldview or the individualistic ontological underpinnings of that view. The state-centric 'prism' (Ashley 1984: 239) remains intact. But it has to be admitted that the material focus of that 'prism' has been altered.

Neorealism may echo realism in asserting the primacy of politics, but many of its articulations do so firmly in the context of political economy. This is clearly demonstrated in the key 1986 volume _Neorealism and its Critics_, edited by Robert Keohane. It could be argued that this collection of essays, which retains its pivotal role in identifying the terms of the critical debate involving neorealism and state-centrism, for the first time placed issues of political economy at the centre of mainstream theoretical exchange in international relations. It is, of course, for the neorealist, a particular kind of political economy, but even in this restricted context it illustrates how the world has changed for the realist, that the growing importance of the global economy, especially to the changing qualities of US power, has challenged the realist view of politics.

It cannot be denied that neorealism ultimately signalled a dilution of the pure power-politics perspective of realism. Increasingly, it has considered such politics in the context of political economy. Interest initially grew in transnationalism, interdependence and vulnerability (Keohane and Nye 1972, 1989; Keohane 1984). A more integrated· approach to the global economy and economic power was adopted. The role of transnational players, including major international organizations and multinational companies, was taken more centrally into consideration, and the concepts of hegemony (Keohane 1984; Gilpin 1987) and regime (Krasner 1983) provided the international frameworks for investigating power in new ways. I will consider a little further the general implications of the neorealist trend with regard to political economy.

If neorealism is caught in its own state-centric conceptual trap, as is being argued here, it has to be recognized that its focus on political economy has highlighted both the contradictory nature of that trap and the imperatives for escaping from it. Even in its own terms, neorealism can be argued to have demonstrated the pressures for opening up the debate about politics and economics, and political and economic power, but its foundational state-centric predispositions have guaranteed a great degree of conceptual closure. Far from contributing to the generation of new ways of thinking about political economy – that is, about the inter-relationship of politics and economics as well as their individual qualities and processes – they have actually worked in a contrary direction by profoundly and extensively entrenching state-centric assumptions. They have actively contributed to keeping closed the ontological circle of state as cause, explanation and end-point of international relations. And they have done so in a specific fashion. By assuming from the start the primacy of politics and the state, they have identified them as hermetically sealed conceptual entities, effectively outlawing a series of fundamental questions about the nature of politics and economics, and their interrelationships in the context of prime categories, including the state.

In defining the ontological parameters of analysis in so strict a state-centric fashion, these dominant approaches *discourage* rather than *encourage* identification, let alone exploration, of these kinds of issue. The power of the contradictions they embrace cannot be underestimated. Surely, in their own terms, it is *illogical* that they should discourage such analytical emphasis. The prominence of the traditions of thought captured by realism and the transformation of its fundamental state-centrism in neorealism affirm the need to investigate the precise means by which such illogicality not only persists, but fails to undermine the apparent *coherence* of these traditions. This can be done only by considering further the nature of theoretical debate in international relations and its implications for the status of state-centrism. This is the subject of part II of the book.

Beyond State-centrism

This part of the book identifies the conceptual challenge in relation to the established structure of debate in international relations and its tendency towards a superficial form of paradigmatism that has served to veil the fundamental paradigmatism of state-centrism. In describing this situation, part II is taking further the critical approach to state-centrism as a dominant form of knowledge. The arguments locate grounds for its endurance in the ways in which different areas of thought in the discipline are divided. The main structure of debate pits each theoretical approach against another as alternative explanatory narratives of the world. This leads to what Ashley has called 'a kind of renaissance carnival' and what I investigate as superficial paradigmatism. This form of paradigmatism takes individual theories as paradigms rather than understanding paradigm as more fundamental and general than that – an expression of assumptions on which analysis is based. State-centrism as assessed in this study represents a fundamental form of paradigmatism.

Superficial paradigmatism, it is argued, provides the environment in which this fundamental paradigmatism can endure. The boundaries of the former counter the kind of collective critical endeavour undertaken in this study, which can bring together and interrelate resources from what are predominantly understood as discrete areas of thought. Feminist perspectives that focus on gender are highlighted as key in this context. Of the three major 'debates' in the discipline (idealism versus realism, history versus science, and positivism versus post-positivism), the third, it is explained, has been characterized by a focus on power and theory, as evidenced, for example, in the work of Ashley and Walker as well as others referred to in this study. But even in the context of the third debate there has been a failure at a general level to interrogate the theoretical hierarchy that continues to *separate* gender analysis from other forms of critique.

Chapter 3 explores the third debate's focus on theory as discourse, and thus on theory as part of social practice. I explain that, similar to all practices, theoretical discourse takes place in time and space, and draws together associations from past and present that link time and space in particular ways. The assumptions of state-centrism, and its central association with the key concept of sovereignty, when interrogated from such a critical standpoint, are highly restrictive in terms of both time and space. State-centrism, as Ashley's and Walker's work especially reveals, locks us conceptually into an eternal present where political identity/subjectivity is mapped in terms of the bounded state as sovereign actor. Craig Murphy and Roger Tooze's Gramscian analysis of the 'orthodoxy' of international political economy charts the development of neorealism as a kind of internationalization of state-centric realism. I discuss in detail their approach and their call for an alternative to orthodoxy – heterodoxy – based on critical exchange and synthesis.

The final section of chapter 3 argues the nature of gender as a radical category in exposing the dominant subjectivities evident in international theory and their relevance to the negotiation of theory as a form of practice. I explain that gender is a radical category in terms of both the fundamental paradigmatism of state-centrism and the superficial paradigmatism that continues to be characteristic of the structure of debate in the discipline of international relations. This discussion locates gender analysis of public/private connections in a spatial context, with a recognition that public and private are spatially defined in various ways, predominant among them those related to the division between home and family (the domestic or personal arena) and the public world beyond. Through this type of analysis, attention is focused on the primary locations of social existence and the ways in which social meanings are generated and maintained in definitions of that existence. Most importantly, efforts are made to break into the patriarchal forces that work towards the representation of society as unified, and actively to undermine the hierarchical opposition of public over private that abstracts the former from the latter.

Chapter 4 examines the role of the normative divide in the structure of debate in international relations, explaining its roots in the so-called first debate in the discipline: idealism versus realism (1920s–1930s). The opening section stresses the importance of historical awareness of the development of realist (state-centric) principles at a time of major conflict between states, the failings of the League of Nations system, World War Two and the subsequent efforts for a new peaceful world order under the intergovernmental umbrella of the United Nations. I argue that with the many reformulations of realism over time, including in neorealism, these principles have become abstracted from the realist/ idealist moment, which Walker, in particular, has identified as pivotal in the history of international theory and of enduring influence. I explain how the realist/utopian opposition has in very real senses placed ethical or normative concerns outside of (beyond) the realist version of politics, and that this version ties the articulation of power, the identity of power, specifically to territorial definitions. Sovereignty is a key concept in this regard, as work by Walker and Ashley reveals. Sovereignty is a conceptual and political category that articulates being in direct relation to space and time but, in the realist mode, in highly particularized fashion.

I examine how sovereignty defines the parameters of being, not only of the political units to which it directly relates – that is, states – but also of the political subjects they contain, on the basis of severance from the global environment, including its human dimension. The next section of chapter 4 develops these points to link spatial understanding to normative issues in the context of critical work on sovereignty. Here I am exploring the relationship between dominant notions of sovereignty and philosophical and spatial universalisms. Critical approaches to sovereignty recognize the ways in which it defines political being or identity directly in terms of territorialization, territorial division. I discuss in detail how Ashley's early research on political economy directly addressed this issue by integrating knowledge processes into his analysis of security. I argue that the critical approaches assessed in this study are seeking to break apart the realist/idealist opposition, to move beyond it. They do so by focusing on, and explaining, the limited political perspective that realist and neorealist state-centrism has maintained, investigating its implications in theory and practice, and offering contrasting, fuller perspectives, including those sensitive to political economy in radical ways.

The partiality of state-centric realist principles involves the exclusion of normative issues as real social forces. I draw on Mervyn Frost's arguments in considering how realist and neorealist framings of politics implicitly and explicitly place normative concerns and influences outside of the realm of real – that is, effective – politics. It is stressed that state-centrism's reduction of politics inherently implies a reductive sense of global space. Its determinism interrelates the spatial and the human via Ashley's notion of the state-centred prism. What we see when we look through this prism is a chain of politics that links states to states, and implicitly within them and via them, as Walker has explained, humans to humans. I depict the critical approaches assessed as working to reclaim politics from realist state-centrism's partial grip and to reformulate understandings of politics and political economy. This reformulation is based on a refusal to treat politics or political economy as static or abstract, and a determination to ground them: treating them as processes involving people operating within territorially defined and spatially structured circumstances, as articulated by discursive as well as more obviously material practices associated with power relations.

For all their differences, including fundamental theoretical ones, these critical approaches share an important quality: the drive for new, non-state-centric forms of comprehending power in global relations. I explain that in straightforward ways they have removed the state from its abstracted role in understanding those relations and placed it actively and firmly back within them. States can be viewed as implicated in, rather than abstracted from, processes of inclusion and exclusion, of social territorialization. The state is problematized as a category or political unit through which human beings should be understood to access the wider world, including other human beings. Territorially and philosophically, it is explained, the state can be seen to have played a prime role, in theory and practice, in expressing separateness. The realist/idealist opposition entrenches this notion of separateness through its partial view of state-centred politics. In reclaiming politics, the critical perspectives assessed are exposing the ways in which normative issues are internal rather than external to politics and political economy. I discuss how this enables active and critical consideration of general issues of inclusion and exclusion, political, economic and cultural.

3 | Beyond Superficial Paradigmatism

The preceding chapters have identified the displacement of state-centrism's distortions as a prime task and have assessed a range of bases for and critiques of them. The central question addressed by this chapter is the *endurance* of the state-centric paradigm, the grounds for it, the collective critical strategy for interrogating it on the basis of treating theory as discourse, and the distinctive role of gender analysis in this regard. In order to explore these issues, it is necessary to refer to a broad overview of the structure of disciplinary debate in international relations.

Three so-called *debates* are generally regarded as capturing key tensions in what are understood to be the general theoretical principles guiding research in the discipline: 'idealism versus realism' (1920s–1930s); 'history versus science' (1950s–1960s); and positivism versus post-positivism (late 1980s).[1] The first debate is rather different from the other two in its broad emphasis on the need to address the conflictual properties of international relations. Its most important historical reference points are the failings of the League of Nations in the interwar period and the outbreak of World War Two. Its role in the development of realism as a dominant school of thought in international relations identifies it as one of the key moments of the discipline's intellectual history. It has enduring influence on normative perspectives on international relations and I will return to these in the next chapter. The second and third debates are similar in that they have concerned more detailed epistemological and methodological issues: that is, the bases of knowledge and the methods for obtaining it. They have also been reflective of wider movements in social study, revolving around the adoption of analytical techniques established in the natural sciences, and more recent challenges to positivism, broadly defined.

The second debate was termed 'the great debate' and set the new scientific principles of the 'behaviouralist' movement against established inductivist methods. The grounds of dispute were mapped out by two articles in *World Politics* in 1966, where Hedley Bull defended the interpretive capacities of traditional approaches to international relations and Morton Kaplan outlined the positive advantages of model building from which general conclusions could be drawn. Kaplan's standpoint was that greater precision could be achieved through the generation and testing of hypotheses. Bull was insistent that there were no grounds for arguing that traditional approaches were imprecise; quite the reverse, as they sought to identify influences relevant to each case or situation under investigation.

I would argue that these essays remain lucid articulations of some of the general theoretical challenges in the study of international relations. For example, the discussion of the risks of mistaking models for reality, whatever the models of analysis may be, remains pertinent; as does the associated question of 'assumptions' that 'are implicit rather than explicit' (Kaplan 1966: 17). Bull's (1966: 363) stress on the US-based character of scientific approaches as distinct from the discipline's British traditions has continued relevance to critical considerations of neorealism's framing of structural rationalities, which were discussed in the previous two chapters (see also Murphy and Tooze 1991a). Bull's (p. 364) urging of serious critique in the face of the strength of the scientific movement evokes the enduring problematic of the need to engage *meaningfully* with powerful theoretical developments.

What has since, however, turned out to be the most spotlighted result of 'the great debate' is the conclusion from various quarters that it was never really any great debate at all (Smith 1995: 17). From the perspective of the arguments advanced in this volume, the detailed aspects of this assessment remain among the most important conclusions about the character of theoretical exchange within the discipline of international relations. They go a long way towards revealing the specific constraints upon its capacities for dynamic conceptualization: that is, conceptualization that remains critical of its own founding assumptions and that develops a flexibility appropriate to its conceptual tasks.

Fundamental versus superficial paradigmatism

Direct criticisms of 'the great debate' uncovered a major contradiction in the discipline, which has yet to be overcome. This contradiction concerns the discipline's claims to conceptualize *international relations* and the prime epistemological and methodological dispositions which have ensured that it is at best predominantly capable of conceptualizing a partial view of international relations, and at worst a highly misleading one. As the previous two chapters have demonstrated, these epistemological and methodological dispositions all relate to the discipline's guiding state-centricity.

John Vasquez's (1983) critique of *The Power of Power Politics* reflected on the fundamental nature of the state-centric paradigm. Utilizing Thomas Kuhn's (1972) influential work on paradigms first published in 1962,[2] and addressing paradigm as *'the fundamental assumptions scholars make about the world they are studying'* (Vasquez 1983: 5), he concludes that the 'behavioural [scientific] revolt' in the study of international relations had neither 'displaced' nor 'seriously challenged' the realist state-centred paradigm (pp. 19–21). Vasquez sums up this paradigm as identifying nation-states and their decision-makers as the means of understanding international relations, dividing domestic and international politics, and restricting the research agenda to the study of 'the struggle for power and peace'.[3]

Vasquez's critique should have sounded an early warning to international relationists that state-centrism was an enduring problematic in terms of the discipline's conceptual constraints. Since his arguments referred to the so-called great debate, they needed to be taken seriously. This study seeks to show that the 'state of the discipline' (Ashley 1991) in the era of 'the third debate' (Lapid 1989) proves that his points were never taken seriously enough. The 'third debate' has featured a multi-faceted attack on the state-centric paradigm, as the previous chapters indicate, but their *joint* force has yet to be felt. This is due to the fact that the predominant structure of disciplinary debate is characterized by what I would identify as *superficial* paradigmatism.

Superficial paradigmatism focuses on particular theories as paradigms, a stance that Vasquez (1983: 4) *à la* Kuhn argued was wrong: a paradigm was much more fundamental and general than that – an expression of assumptions upon which analysis was based. Vasquez made this point clearly and forcefully, but an eradication of the more superficial form of paradigmatism in the discipline has failed to follow. Richard Ashley (1991: 38) has been among those to critique most dramatically this form's qualities, its 'territorialising logic'. Students are confronted with the option of selecting alternative paradigms: Marxism, liberalism, realism and so on.

> Each is presented to the student as a state of the discipline in itself – a state that has its central perspective, its true subject of history, its territorial domain, its master narrative, its aims, its external problems still to be

resolved. And each is presented as a basis upon which other paradigms can be judged and shown to be misrepresentations, parodies, or games of interpretation having their objectified rules, not the certain origins of truth their exponents take them to be. (p. 46)

Ashley portrays this as 'a kind of Renaissance carnival'. While this carnival of superficial paradigmatism goes on, the more serious business of dealing with the fundamental paradigmatism of state-centrism is left to one side. And the theoretical boundaries articulated by the dominant form of superficial paradigmatism counter the kind of collective critique undertaken in this study, one which brings together connecting critical engagements from approaches that are generally regarded as distinct or separate.

Just like the so-called great debate, 'the inter-paradigm debate' (Hoffman 1987) is in any genuine sense no debate at all (Smith 1995: 18–20). It is much more a statement of contrasting theoretical positions generally treated in discrete 'territorial' fashion than a meaningful exchange of interacting ideas and approaches. This is somewhat paradoxical in the case of the third debate, which overtly places power/ knowledge issues on the agenda, as evidenced, for example, in the critiques of state-centrism discussed by this study. The problem with the third debate is the limitations on its application of its critical perspectives on power and theory. It has failed so far, for example, thanks to the effectiveness of superficial paradigm boundaries, to interrogate sufficiently deeply its own theoretical hierarchy that separates gender analysis from other forms of critique. Sandra Whitworth (1989) was correct when she described this recently as 'alarming'.

> For feminists concerned with developing an international relations theory which is sensitive to gender, the continued silence of critical international relations in relation to gender presents a fundamental challenge, perhaps even more so than from within the mainstream of international relations. Realism, for example, has been accused of a variety of 'absences', not least of which is its inability to theorise its own central unit of analysis, the state. Within this context, an ability or unwillingness to theorise about gender does not seem so unusual. However, critical international relations purports to contemplate the social and political complex as a whole and to understand the process of change within both the whole and its parts. In this context, the failure to acknowledge, let alone analyse, the character and bases of female subordination within both the study and practice of international relations is untenable. (p. 265)

Whitworth has rightly identified the future challenge as being represented by the achievement of international relations theory that is '*both* critical _and_ feminist' (p. 270). It is part of the substance of that challenge which this study addresses. Its complexities will be explored by considering theory as discourse and by linking gender critiques specifically to questions of spatiality, which can be identified as key concerns beyond state-centrism.

Theory as discourse

One of the most powerful qualities of 'the third debate' has been the identification of theory as discourse and extensive examination of its meanings, including notably in relation to state-centrism. Treating theory as discourse is to recognize it as a form of practice directly relevant to understanding power.[4] It requires an awareness of the degree to which theoretical discourse is embedded in social practices more generally. Similar to all practices, it takes place in time and space, and draws together associations from past and present that link time and space in particular ways. Treating theoretical discourse as material practice requires distance from abstract notions of knowledge processes as mystically passed through texts, and impels the capture of _timeless ideas_ that float free from spatial links. It requires a literal _grounding_ of critical considerations of knowledge, and thus the posing of all the kinds of questions about it that would be addressed to other practices. Why and where has it been produced, for what purposes, and how have these changed over time; who uses it, how and for what purposes; to whom is it addressed, how and with what results; what does it reveal or obscure and why?

These are just some of the questions and, of course, they are all concerned with power. Addressing them requires looking at not only specific discourses, but their wider connections in theory and practice. Thus examinations of discourses in the study of international relations and international political economy have drawn on broader issues of discourse and power. Michael Shapiro (1989) has stressed, as have Richard Ashley (see, in particular, 1987 and 1989) and Rob Walker (1993) in a range of detailed ways, that we need to recognize politics as taking place in a world where its dominant meanings have already been generated and thus where there is an 'intimate relationship between textual practices and politics' (Shapiro 1989: 13). Textuality in the study of the social sciences introduces insights from literary theory, recognizing that texts should be analysed in relation to one another as well as their social contexts. The notion of intertextuality explicitly identifies the 'codes' and 'conventions' that influence the production of texts and connect them

(p. 11). When theory is regarded as part of these textual practices, one can begin to see how such an approach counters abstract notions of theory and works to deobjectify it, to assert it as part of the *historical* processes of human power relations that have brought us from a past to a present, and which, without critical interventions, may carry us forward to a particular kind of future.

The issue of history is crucial here because such critical work is forthrightly, if not always overtly, urging the adoption of a multidimensional sense[5] of time and space, one that recognizes the interaction of knowledge and other practices in spatially defined locations – states, of course, being a prime, and in the case of IR probably *the* prime, category. This work is countering a linear, one-dimensional approach to history, which tends to sever considerations of it from spatial linkages, or, at least, to fail to make explicit those issues associated with connections between time and space that influence our specific understanding of the very nature of historical developments themselves. Via these critiques, time can no longer be dealt with as dislocated from space: the precise ways in which time/space relations are articulated, including through knowledge processes, are of direct interest. It is important to stress that the move away from abstraction thus implied relates to a combination of time and space, requiring more material thought about each, about their interconnections and the role of knowledge processes in contributing to their formation and maintenance.

Shapiro and Neaubauer's (1990: 99) explanation of the problematic in their investigation of 'spatiality and policy discourse' is helpful here:

> The shape of a society's spaces – leisure space, work space, public space, military space – tends to remain largely implicit for a variety of reasons. One is, of course, the relatively long duration of that shaping process so that few can discern a process of actual boundary shaping or movement. However, part of the inattention to spatial predicates of policy discourse is positively administered. Dominant forms of social theory, for example both liberal and Marxist, fail, with some exceptions, to encode the spatial dimensions of human association. For the dominant tendencies in both these theoretical traditions, *space is either natural or neutral*; it is either the empty arena within which political association and contention develop or it is the sanctified, historically destined places whose boundaries and internal configurations should remain inviolable.
>
> There are good reasons to resist this naturalizing of space. At a minimum, a careful attention to the irredeemably contextual contribution of a speaker or writer's situation to the meaning of the utterances should suggest why. *Intelligibility is intimately connected to standing, to the sites and locations from which meanings are shaped.* And, the spaces from which dis-

course is produced are just as much constituted as sets of practices as the discourses themselves; social relations thus form a complex in which topological and discursive practices are inseparable. [my emphases][6]

The critiques of state-centrism discussed in this study recognize states as historically created and key loci of politics and thus political subjectivity, _and_, importantly, state-centric discourses as intrinsic rather than extrinsic to – that is, a material rather than an abstract part of – _the process of politics_. The term 'politics' here is clearly being used in a sense extending well beyond institutional definitions of its forms and practices, government and its operations at various levels. It incorporates theory as practice (rather than abstracting it from practice) and thus makes it central to understanding history. Bringing history back into the picture has been a general feature of the critiques of state-centrism introduced. It is a major characteristic of the drive of these critiques against the tyranny of abstraction maintained by dominant forms of state-centrism. It is not enough to assert that such abstraction exists and that it presents problematics. These problematics must be spelled out and exposed in great detail before their full import can be recognized.

Work by Richard Ashley and Rob Walker has collectively done much to reveal and attack the precise qualities of state-centric abstractions. Their endeavours, in common with gender critiques, have been enormously complex and serve as proof in principle of what can lie behind seemingly straightforward assumptions about the world. Their critiques transfer attention from state-centrism's claims to knowledge about the world to the foundations on which such claims are based. They historicize and politicize state-centric international theory and thus provide a rich contextualization of its principles and orientations. Their work offers important clues to the nature of the relationship between international theory and international practice, and illuminates strategies for breaking the conceptual grip of state-centrism. Their writings shed light on state-centric discourse's locations in theory and practice, and see states as historically formed social collectivities that address issues of individual and social identity as sovereign in ways that are far from immediately evident. In assessing their work, one is removed from the empty abstract category of the state, which has dominated the field of international relations for too long, and placed in a position where pursuing the grounds for that domination and the reasons for escaping it are priorities.

What is distinctive about their writings with respect to the critical interests of this study is their close attention to the conceptual architecture of the state-centric tradition: _state-as-sovereign-actor_ and _order_ in an *anarchic* world. They probe interrelationships between the theory and practice of this worldview, and they do so in ways that are particularly powerful with regard to possibilities for new conceptualizations of global relations. They provide means for dismantling this architecture and for examining its various supporting structures, and explain why we should move beyond such frameworks for thinking about the world. These are *meaningful* and *strategic* offerings. This statement is simple but vital: once again in common with gender critiques, they play a crucial role in developing the debate about state-centrism to the point where the state-as-abstract-category can no longer be tolerated. They have concretized the state as it appears in dominant discourses of international relations and they have done so by processes that specifically undermine the very terms of the tradition of state-centrism.

Central to the mystique of coherence which surrounds that tradition are the concepts of security, identity and individuality. *States as secure, individual units with sovereign identities have been personified implicitly and explicitly as rational man writ large.* Ashley's (1989) discussion of 'logocentric'/dualistic discourse (introduced in chapter 1) emphasizes the importance of 'historicity' and helps in understanding the procedures by which such discourse works to efface it. Spatial and temporal dimensions are introduced here with the concepts of 'presence' and 'absence', which the dualistic structures, in complementing and reinforcing one another, assert. Discourse is linked to issues of subjectivity and time and place. Subjectivity is established on the basis of this 'presence' and 'absence'. For example, the dominant subjectivity of man is dependent on the absence of woman and is supported by the complementary and associated theme of rationality (and the absence of irrationality), and so on. This form of discourse is inherently abstract. In order to assert the 'sovereign voice' as 'a pure and *extrahistorical* presence' (my emphasis), it lifts the subject out of time and political space where difference exists.

> Given an undecidable diversity of contesting interpretive possibilities, a logocentric discourse is inclined to impose closure by resorting to one or another fixed standard of interpretation that is itself accorded the status of a pure and identical presence – a standpoint and standard supposedly occupying a place outside of history and beyond politics from which it is possible to give voice to a singular interpretation of the historical and political differences perceived. (p. 262)

Theory is one of the most powerful forms of discourse owing to the importance of its rhetorical content and its level of self-referentiality.

Nevertheless, if it is understood as discourse then it can be subjected to logocentric interrogation. This is helpful at least in a heuristic manner when considering superficial paradigmatism. Theoretical discourse is dependent on the assertion of a 'pure presence', a 'sovereign voice'. The power of individual theories is based on the degree to which they can successfully make their own claims without reference to different kinds of theoretical challenge. The most powerful theories would be understood to be those with the strongest historical achievements of this kind.

In this context, Craig Murphy and Roger Tooze (1991a), in their examination of the 'orthodoxy' of international political economy, chart the development of neorealism as a kind of internationalization of realism. In this way, their critique parallels neorealism's focus on hegemony[7] as an internationalized transformation of the understanding of power common to the power politics stance of realism. While most are aware of the key role that the concept of hegemony plays among both neorealists and their critics (Keohane 1986a, 1989; Gilpin 1987), surprisingly little has been said about why this is the case, especially in the context of neorealism itself. Murphy and Tooze could not emphasize more strongly the interrelationship between theory and practice. They paint a picture in which the post-1945 Bretton Woods system[8] internationalized the realist approach to economics as separate from politics, subject to technical control and principally about wealth maximization. But, they explain, between 1968 and 1971, when the US role in the Bretton Woods structure and thus the structure itself collapsed significantly, 'the interests of the US government and those of the liberal system as a whole began to diverge' (Murphy and Tooze 1991b: 3). The search for 'new technical rules and norms' led to 'a process of _relinking_ the studies of IR [international relations], economics and politics' (p. 4). They stress that the approach worked to maintain two key distinctions: between economics and politics, and between the national and the international (p. 4).

The return to relative calm in the later 1980s, and an accompanying theoretical complacency, have led to the 'consolidation' of the 'orthodoxy', in their view. Murphy and Tooze's (1991a: 9) subsequent comment that this orthodoxy must be understood as 'a fusion of theory and practice – as a social product' is a useful encapsulation of the points explored above. They explain orthodoxy as 'a particular mode of production of IPE [international political economy] knowledge' (Murphy and Tooze 1991a: 13). Here they capture the idea of knowledge processes as material in the broadest sense of that term. They argue that production of the kinds of paradigm discussed above takes place within a larger positivist epistemological and ontological framework, which 'sees knowledge production as purely an intellectual process' abstracted from the social circumstances understood to be its 'object' (p. 14). The positivistic *'culture* of orthodoxy' is important rather than its individual paradigms: 'This culture has its material base, and it encompasses not only the production and dissemination of knowledge, but, critically, also the creation of consensus around or upon the knowledge so produced' (p. 14).

Murphy and Tooze's use of the concept of a 'culture of orthodoxy' illuminates the importance of considering not only the production of knowledge, but also its *reception* and *acceptance* as part of understanding its processes as material.[9] Their use of the notion 'common sense' as descriptive of the status of 'orthodoxy' can helpfully be understood only in direct relation to this point. The idea concerns what is considered to be assumed, to go without question, in particular social contexts. The theoretical parameters of the orthodoxy, notably positivism and methodological individualism, define its 'common sense' (Murphy and Tooze 1991a: 17–23).

The analysis by Murphy and Tooze bears characteristics common to other critiques of realism/neorealism discussed above. I will highlight here only aspects that represent important embellishments or developments, particularly with regard to the study of international political economy. They stress, in Gramscian fashion, the role of the 'acceptance' of economic techno-rationalism in the post-1945 global economy as the means by which 'legitimate economic knowledge and legitimate political action' have come to be defined (p. 18), crucially: 'Acceptance also externalized the system of meaning from the dominant state(s) into an objective part of the external reality faced by the participants: *it became just as real as the material conditions facing them*' (p. 18, my emphasis). The orthodoxy cannot address 'the reality of intersubjective meaning in the structure of the global political economy'; nor, because of its positivistic ontology, can it account for 'its own emergence and purpose' (pp. 18–19). The orthodoxy depicts knowledge as the unproblematic pursuit of 'truth' and cannot recognize 'the reciprocal interaction of meaning and material capability' that is the global political economy (p. 19).

Murphy and Tooze identify an unsatisfactory partial approach to ideology as part of reality in the orthodoxy's 'contesting ideologies' structure. The orthodoxy's positivist base, they argue, prevents ideology from being understood in any deep material sense, and therefore gives it a 'contradictory' status as an analytical tool (pp. 22–3). In discussing the 'universe' of orthodox IPE, they depict a static, ahistorical attitude towards the relationship between politics and economics – 'one clearly derived from the political and ideological influences of liberalism in the eighteenth and nineteenth centuries' (p. 24). Their critique of this assumed relationship has parallels with Richard Ashley's (1983, 1984) assessment of neorealism's 'economism', discussed in the previous chapter. Murphy and Tooze depict the relationship as one in which economics is clearly the higher rational form of human organization and politics is the realm that fills in the social gaps, or, as they put it, '"politics" takes place where the realm of economics stops' (p. 24). They are also firm about the US-centric nature of the orthodoxy, arguing that it clearly reflects US government concerns linked to post-1945 US 'global supremacy' and 'challenges' to it (p. 24).[10] This affects the way certain issues, such as trade, are 'privileged' (pp. 25–6).

Murphy and Tooze's solution to the problem of the 'culture of orthodoxy' is in some ways an oppositional one that does not fundamentally disrupt superficial paradigmatism's competing paradigms framework. They posit an alternative 'culture' of heterodoxy in which participants share both a disruptive stance towards the orthodoxy's fundamental positivism and a commitment to 'openness'. This is characteristic of the general orientation of 'the third debate' and is depicted by these authors as 'the emerging new international political economy' (p. 30). Their emphasis on critical conversation and 'honest attempts at synthesis' in certain respects could be regarded as supportive of the kind of endeavour undertaken in this study. However, the position developed here in this respect has two major underlying themes. The first is that the problematics of such synthesis require more overt attention, a process to which this study aims to contribute. The second is that gender critiques in their deep approaches to the social relations of power offer distinctive means for assisting understanding of these problematics and for moving beyond them.

Gender as radical category

I will continue the central interest of this chapter in theory as discourse, in seeing theory as part of practice. Gender critiques have provided the most all-encompassing assessment of theory _as_ discourse and thus theory _as_ practice to date. They have extensively investigated the ways in which the 'presence' of men and male-dominated interests and the 'absence' of women and their interests have characterized theory (see, for example, Peterson 1992a, 1992b; Peterson and Runyan 1993; Sylvester 1994). This is, of course, a fairly broad-brush description, but it nevertheless reflects the holistic thrusts of this crucial critical work, especially for awareness of the importance of understanding discourse in connection with power. One of the major strengths of this work in critical regards is its strong purchase on both the historical influence of dominant theoretical traditions *and* their interaction with other dominant forms of social practice.

There are a number of key issues in this respect. These critiques explore the dominant subjectivities evident in international theory and the ways in which these are *reflective of*, and *assertive of*, dominant subjectivities in the various practices of international relations. They draw attention directly to theoretical discourse as implicated in historical processes, and thus to understanding discourse as a material part of social relations. One of the most dramatic insights extensively offered by this body of critical work, reflecting a wide range of interests, is that theoretical work, far from being abstracted from practice, is a form of practice that has had and continues to have profound influence on awareness of the 'absence' of women and their interests in policy realms of politics and economics, and the ways in which dominant discourses, including theoretical ones, work to maintain such 'absences' (Tickner 1992).

Here we come to the question of how a developed approach to discourse and power directs attention to the workings of logocentric dualisms as *discursive practices over time*. Such an approach encourages attention to how such practices work to effect power, and thus they assist in understanding power as dynamic rather than static. The presences and absences revealed in logocentric analysis are completely misunderstood unless regarded in terms of process. Such terms are relevant to understanding strategies that work to counter dominant forms of power *as well as* strategies that work to maintain such power (Foucault 1971, 1982). This is a crucial point regarding discourse and the investigation of power in the context of theory. The power of theory is interpreted not as necessarily fixed, but as contingent, open to challenge and to reassertion, possibly in modified form.

Gender critiques are, in this sense, unashamedly political in their character and are themselves strategies, on varying bases, for countering dominant forms of male-centred theory. It cannot be stressed enough that such critiques are a sophisticated expression of theory *as practice*, of theory *as political practice*. They have a great deal to teach about the implication of dominant subjectivities in discourses, and about broad and enduring processes of reinforcement *across* discourses. And, as the above points indicate, they link discourse to time and space. In investigating the nature of *politics* and *political economy* in predominantly state-centred theory, they assist awareness of the specificities and partialities of this theory. And, equally importantly, they press home the continuing effects of them as implicated in, not abstracted from, practice.

The superficial paradigmatism of 'the third debate' continues to reflect socially institutionalized gender hierarchies in failing to take deep account of gender issues and the kinds of critical question about gender relations, including as embedded in various knowledge practices, indicated by feminist theoretical perspectives. Gender remains a radical category in relation to both the fundamental paradigmatism of state-centrism and the superficial paradigmatism that continues to be characteristic of the structure of theoretical debate in the discipline of international relations. The superficial separation of gender critiques in 'the third debate' draws attention away from rather than towards the deeper implications of these perspectives for the debate as a whole. Gender and the public/private hierarchies associated with it are considerations _implicit_ or _ignored_ in forms of analysis that fail to take account of them in explaining power.

Much of 'the third debate' has been intensely theoretical in its anti-positivistic turns in seeking to unravel power/knowledge questions. But in many ways it has failed to interrogate itself in this precise critical context. It has therefore demonstrated a partial critical nature, one that operates predominantly with public/private hierarchies as given, in theoretical as well as other forms of social practice, and one that opens up issues of subjectivity, but does so on a similarly restricted basis. The connections between public and private, between public and private subjectivities, are left largely unexplored. Questions of political and economic space are opened up, but, significantly, as if their dynamics can be primarily understood in terms of the 'presence' of the public and the 'absence' of the private. The power relations and the dominant knowledges associated with them are taken as given to the extent that the individual is assumed as _man_ or hu_man_, and is thus addressed as present in the public sphere. The critique of politics, such as it is, remains generally bounded by these parameters.

The approach of this study is in tension, therefore, with Jim George's (1994: 28) view that 'genuine space for critical self-reflection and for other ways of knowing and Being' must be opened up partly 'so [in order] that the International Relations community in general might become more able to take advantage of perspectives such as feminism'. This stance does not, in my view, offer appropriate strategic status to feminist perspectives. My arguments demonstrate grounds for considering them rather as vital to the possibilities for opening up such space, as offering distinctive and necessary paths towards more adequate and dynamic conceptualizations of global relations, paths which cannot be discovered by critical routes that perceive politics and economics, agency and structure, through the partialities of the patriarchal prism.

If gender can be considered a radical category then this study argues that this is so because of the qualities of its theory/practice purchase, particularly because of the fresh spatial vistas it offers for investigating social relations of power within and across national boundaries. Importantly, it offers the possibility of escape from *a gender-neutral sense of spatiality* (Youngs forthcoming). To treat social space as gender-neutral is to fail to take account of how institutionalized forms of power and practice, most notably as revealed by public/private divisions, hierarchically define it specifically in terms of gender. Space and power, or rather the specificities of space and power, have always been central to gender analysis. Feminists have long illustrated how men and women, male and female as categories, have been socially produced and reproduced in relation to the divisions between the public and private.[11] As processes of struggle and emancipation as well as oppression grow in complexity, the value of greater precision in understanding the nature of public and private increases too. One of the strengths of the feminist public/private critique is that it overtly associates power relations with particular definitions of social spaces and activities. As a strategy it encourages attention to the primary locations of social existence and the ways in which social meanings are generated and maintained in the organization of that existence. It seeks to break into the patriarchal forces that work towards the representation of society as unified, and actively undermines the hierarchical opposition of public over private that abstracts the former from the latter. In order to understand gender inequalities and gendered identities, it is essential to investigate how they are constructed *across* public/private divides.

The orientation of feminist critique, in exposing the dynamics of public/private power relations, in disrupting the presence of the public based on an absence[12] of the private, aims towards a new spatial ontology in social analysis, explicitly locating the relationship of politics and economics in the context of the socially and spatially constructed relationships between public and private.[13] Ontology operates at the most fundamental level conceptually; it shapes the parameters of potential insight and analysis. With regard to dominant ontological standpoints, this involves assumptions that have been legitimized *over time* to the point where they become hidden or gain an apparently non-negotiable status. The crystallized overtones of the prism are helpful for capturing the nature of patriarchal perspectives, suggesting rigidity of viewpoint as well as an indication of this having hardened over time into 'common sense'. Feminist frameworks offer the conceptual tools to shatter the patriarchal prism, but as 'the third debate' illustrates, due account must be taken of the obstacles to this possibility. There may be a centuries-old tradition of feminist theorizing about the public/private, but because this form of theorizing has always been, in important respects, marginal, it remains largely invisible and ineffective; it lacks historical force in the context of mainstream patriarchal discourses of politics and political economy. As Spike Peterson (1996: 18) has put it: 'masculinist ways of knowing marginalize women as agents and gender as an analytic category'.

Thus even the task of making gender an *effective* category critically and analytically remains a major challenge, one that this study seeks to contribute to address. Its focus on discourse and power is an integrated facet of that challenge, particularly in relation to understanding social space. Its focus on theoretical discourse as a form of practice, as inter-active with and directly relevant to assessments of other forms of prac-tice, including importantly those that have become institutionalized over time, is essential in this regard. Abstract and reductionist state-centrism with its assumed stance towards spatiality, its significantly empty notion of social space as bounded territory, is an influential patriarchally driven form of knowledge about the world, a theoretical discourse that *reflects* and *reinforces*, among other things, assumptions that the social constructions of gender and their widespread manifestations and rami-fications are not essential to understanding power in the world. Buried beneath state-centrism's collapsing of agency and structure is a funda-mental assumption, all the more important for its deep (that is, historic-ally embedded) nature, that there is no need to take account of gender in defining those categories. Through the patriarchal prism, the world can be viewed in its principally public guise. It is a world abstracted from public/private gendered dynamics, one where the rational man writ large is the given means of understanding both agency and struc-ture, and, crucially, their interactions.

The rational-man-writ-large perspective provides an abstract approach to agency and structure on the bases outlined in the preceding two chap-ters. The state as rational man writ large provides an abstract approach to the state itself, as also outlined. In key respects the rational man as unit of analysis is a reductive and abstract means of understanding even the notion of agent. The approach to discourse explored in this chapter is highly disruptive of such forms of abstraction owing to its attempts analytically to *locate* agency/structure processes and indeed agents within their material, social and institutionalized settings. Material in this context, as stressed already, incorporates the discursive realm ar-ticulated in specific varieties of discourse related, for example, to differ-ent areas of diplomacy (Der Derian 1991), politics (Shapiro 1989; Hennessy 1993; J. George 1994) and economics (Johnston 1991; Harcourt 1994; Elson 1995) in various forms, written, spoken and transmitted. A close focus on discourse and power inevitably brings with it a distinctive sensitivity to agency/structure interactions because it directly links differentiated expressions of, or resistances to, *social* norms or values to individual subjects or groups of them.

> language, in the form of socially and historically specific discourses, cannot have any social and political effectivity except in and through the actions of the individuals who become its bearers by taking up the forms of subjectivity and the meanings and values which it proposes and acting upon them. The individual is both the site for a range of possible forms of subjectivity and, at any particular moment of thought or speech, a subject, subjected to the regime of meaning of a particular discourse and enabled to act accordingly. . . . Language and the range of subject positions which it offers always exists in historically specific discourses which inhere in social institutions and practices and can be organized analytically in discursive fields. (Weedon 1987: 34–5)

Discourse analysis of the kind undertaken in this study recognizes the *production of meanings and values* as intrinsic to social relations of power and understanding subjectivities in that context. The next chapter explores how problematic such an approach is in the context of the normative divide perpetuated by dominant state-centrism, and indicates how critiques of state-centrism signal the analytical urgency of moving beyond it. Gender analysis is significant for the *breadth and depth*, socially and spatially, of its focus on the production of meanings and values, and thus subjectivities, as will be explored further in part III.

4 | Beyond the Normative Divide

Politics are made up of two elements – utopia and reality – belonging to two different planes which can never meet. There is no greater barrier to clear political thinking than failure to distinguish between ideals, which are utopia, and institutions, which are reality. (Carr 1946 (1939): 93)

The characteristic feature of the crisis of the twenty years between 1919 and 1939 was the abrupt descent from the visionary hopes of the first decade to the grim despair of the second, from a utopia which took little account of reality to a reality from which every element of utopia was rigorously excluded. (p. 224)

Reading E. H. Carr's *The Twenty Years' Crisis 1919–1939*, from which the above quotes are taken, remains an apt way to steep oneself in one of the most enduring problematics of international relations in theory and practice: the dichotomy of the ideal and the real. This chapter considers how this dichotomy, which characterized the first major conceptual shift in the discipline's relatively short history, endures as an intellectual and historically rooted motif imprinted on efforts to consider global relations. The two quotes above remind us of the intricate way in which philosophical preoccupations in the study of international relations have been intertwined with the aspirations and devastation of the most hopeful and terrible events of human history. The idealist/realist shift signalled just how practice-oriented a discipline international relations was, and is, and the degree to which those operating within it could not afford to ignore the most difficult issues associated with the practices and outcomes of politics, including those which lead to extreme forms of human conflict.

The realist tradition in international relations, its principles and its orientations, can be fully understood only when contextualized within the times in which it was formed: those of the failure of the interwar hopes for international peace through the League of Nations and the outbreak and conduct of World War Two. The realist worldview was asserted at a time when a large part of the world was paying the price for what was perceived as an overemphasis on the ideal and an under-emphasis on the real, the issue of power (p. vii); hence the power politics approach, the desire to perceive the world from the states*man*'s stand-point, to draw back from grand global views and to focus on the interior motivations of the political units in charge of the weapons of war: states. Hans J. Morgenthau's *Politics Among Nations: the struggle for power and peace* remains the most comprehensive and familiar statement of realist tenets, but the fact that it has run into six editions too often obscures that it was first published in 1948 (Morgenthau and Thompson 1985).

One of the most interesting essays a student of any level of experience might be asked to write on this text would be a reflection on the rele-vance of its timing. The endurance of realist principles and their domin-ance in state-centric traditions has the tendency to disconnect them too strongly from their historical roots, which reveal a great deal about theory/practice elements of their orientation. The realist story has been told and retold in many forms,[1] but it is still hard to make total sense of its own terms outside of a sensitivity to the times in which it took hold as a mainstream approach to international relations. It is important to recognize and to stress that realism is not just a theory; it is a reaction to a historical moment of major world conflict (Olson and Groom 1991: 104–29). In important senses, formulations and reformulations of real-ism, including within neorealism, echo that historical moment pro-foundly, but they do so implicitly, often in ways that are unnoticed or forgotten.[2]

Chapter 1 discussed the unexpected traces that can be considered to link today's realist notions of sovereignty to more ancient understandings of it via founding texts such as Hobbes's (1968 (1651)) *Leviathan*. The specific effects or roles of such traces are extremely difficult to assess, but they should not be ignored. However, the established structure of theoretical debate in international relations, as discussed in the previ-ous chapter, has tended to veil them. Thus drawing out the complexity of realism's historical roots in relation to theory and practice has been a major focus of much critical writing in the discipline in recent times, including much of that examined in this study.[3] The main purpose has been to contribute to understanding the bases of the power of realism as a form of theory, to expand awareness of its links to practice and to indicate how its 'historically constituted tensions, contradictions and evasions' might be considered (Walker 1993: 106; see also Ashley 1984).

The realist/idealist moment

Rob Walker (1993: 107) has identified the realist/idealist moment in the history of international theory as a pivotal and enduring influence. It is a key foundational element of his analysis of the 'inside/outside' character of the dominant sovereignty-bound thinking in the discipline. For Walker, the dichotomy between political realism and utopianism is 'the grand opposition' that has worked to reduce the complexity of 'historical traditions and philosophical positions' associated with it. He depicts it as a 'polarity' that is 'something like a founding myth'. The significance of his assessment of this myth is multidimensional and of particular interest to those wishing to advance the study of international relations to a more comprehensive analysis of global relations. Walker's thesis addresses international theory in relation to space and time, interrogating how sovereignty as a political concept, mobilized in dominant state-centric approaches, incorporates a particularized interpretation of territory and history. Because Walker is addressing theories of sovereignty as aspects of the practices of sovereignty, his approach inherently problematizes the understanding of the whole realm of politics. Where does politics begin and end? What does it mean to study politics, if theory is understood to be integral to it? These are the kinds of question that Walker's orientation prompts. Clearly it expands awareness of the types of issue to be addressed in negotiating the dynamics of politics.

His emphasis on the realist/idealist or utopian opposition involves a direct consideration of the distorted qualities of politics as formulated in dominant forms of state-centric theorizing. The realist/ utopian opposition has in very real senses placed ethical or normative concerns *outside* or *beyond* the realist version of politics, and this version ties the articulation of power, the identity of power, as it were, specifically to territorial definitions. As Walker has explored, sovereignty is the key category incorporating the linkages between territory, identity and power. Increasingly, owing to this kind of critical analysis, sovereignty can be seen as the definitive transmissionary category in dominant state-centred thinking. It is fundamental to predominant realist definitions of political essence or being as indicative of divisions between 'inside' and 'outside', as dependent on territorially bounded state identity (Youngs 1997b).

This is highly significant for theorists wishing to address global relations from within the discipline of international relations, for they must negotiate the conceptual pitfalls that this situation creates. The issue of attempts to reclaim politics from the restricted parameters of main-stream state-centred thinking must be given serious consideration. This is because such thinking inherently associates politics with a specific form of territorialization, and eternalizes that depiction via the power ful concept of sovereignty. This ultimately realist encapsulation of world politics has managed to maintain its neatly sealed logic as a frame-work of analysis largely because of the realist/idealist opposition that the structure of debate in international theory has maintained. The conceptualization of sovereignty as it is associated with mainstream state-centric thought thus has a great deal to answer for.

This returns to this study's earlier discussions of agency, for the points being made here about a restrictive definition of politics and the role of sovereignty must be considered in this regard. It assists critical negoti-ation of the mystique of sovereignty, the breaking of its mystical cover. It is possible to learn more about the hidden meanings of sovereign be-ing, the nature of 'autonomy' (Walker 1993: 111). It is possible to un-cover its partial qualities resulting from the idealist/realist opposition, which delimits realist politics along specifically anti-idealist or anti-utopian lines, thus effectively casting out a balanced inclusion of 'ethical' considerations (pp. 50–80). In this lies the importance of normative ap-proaches to international relations, which have, in certain senses, com-pensated for the omissions of realism in this regard. These approaches are rich and varied,[4] and draw significantly on the post-Enlightenment emphasis on universal notions such as equality and rights (pp. 59–60). There is undoubtedly an important polarity between realist and norma-tive stances, which the kind of analysis Walker has undertaken suggests should be probed more deeply. There are ways in which the impact of this oppositional framework has been veiled by the traditional assess-ments of 'international society' or 'society of states', which are largely forms of modified realism.[5]

Hedley Bull's (1977) depiction of 'anarchical society' has become prob-ably the most familiar among these assessments, and seeks to explore what might be considered the cohesive qualities of anarchy.[6] But such interpretations do not go beyond the state-centric paradigm of realism in ontological or methodological terms. Neither do they deal effectively with the kinds of resulting problematic that this study has investigated. The complex connections made by Walker's critique of sovereignty, however, do offer helpful conceptual tools. Rather than go further into the extensive and detailed arguments put forward by Walker (1993), I will draw out the general nature of the connections he makes and con-sider some of their implications.

Walker's approach presents a multidimensional understanding of power, in asserting sovereignty as a conceptual and political category that articulates being in direct relation to space and time. It highlights the particularized ways in which 'sovereign identity' as expressed in mainstream thinking in international relations links 'space and time' (p. 9). A key factor in this process is the denial of fundamental human/human and human/environment interdependence, of which Richard Ashley (1980) has argued there should be awareness. The opposition between states, and implicitly their subjects or citizens, and the universal or global in human and environmental respects is maintained via the conceptual and political category of sovereignty, which asserts identity strictly in terms of separateness, in terms of divisions between 'inside' and 'outside'. Sovereignty thus defines the parameters of being, not only of the political units to which it directly relates – that is, states – but also of the political subjects they contain, on the basis of severance from the global environment, including its human dimension.

Such conceptualizations serve to abstract the state from time, from people and from the dynamics of the practices that work to support and contest it (Walker 1993: 168). The state becomes 'a formal and almost lifeless category' and major questions such as the vast 'variety of state forms' are left unexplored (p. 168; see also Jackson 1993). Embedded in such an approach is an understanding of the politics of identity rigidly channelled through the state, a politics that crudely opposes the insider to the outsider along the lines of presence and absence already discussed (Walker 1993: 174). Such a conceptual position fundamentally assumes the very nature of humanity as well as that of politics, themes articulated powerfully throughout the body of Walker's work.[7] His arguments have focused on both state-centred reductions of understandings of political identity and humanity, and the tensions between the global threats of, for example, nuclear weaponry or environmental destruction and sovereign notions of security. These arguments have sought to disrupt the 'limits' of contemporary 'political imagination' (1990, 1993: ix), to challenge state-centred interpretations of humanity and politics in international relations (Youngs 1996b), to get beyond the point where 'state sovereignty affirms that we have our primary – often over-riding – political identity as participants in a particular community, but retain a potential connection with "humanity" through participation in a broader international system' (Walker 1993: 154).

This study has stressed in various ways the problems of abstraction embedded in dominant state-centrism. Walker's framework for understanding global relations deeply disrupts such abstraction via the conceptual linkages identified here. These reveal the full force of dominant state-centrism's ontological distortions, the all-encompassing nature of its processes of abstraction. This has implications for structure and agency issues, the collapsing of which through realist and neorealist moves has resulted in a flat and undynamic conceptualization of global relations, one that narrows interpretation of politics as process to strictly state-centred terms.

The task of the critical work assessed in this book has largely been to tear open that view of global relations, to reintroduce the possibility of dynamic approaches to structure and agency that recognize their historically contextualized interactivity. This helps in seeing states not as static, but as constantly emergent entities that cannot easily be interpreted on the basis of segregated notions of politics and economics. These critiques have thrown out the simplistic hierarchy of 'levels of analysis', where the conceptual framework for analysing international relations links states in a linear fashion to the international. They have sought to create quite a different spatial sense of global relations, implicitly as well as explicitly; one in which states are not reduced to their external actions or supposed motivations. Walker's perspective plays a particular role in highlighting the deepest aspects of these crucial, critical developments in the discipline.

Spatial understanding and normative issues

In probing states as political process, in assessing sovereignty's spatial dependency and its claims to eternity as a category of political identity, Walker's conceptual standpoint launches a distinctive all-out attack on dominant state-centrism's static worldview. It indicates comprehensively the imperatives for historical *and* spatial sensitivities in the study of global relations, and implicates them directly in the understanding of politics. The last point is essential to the enhancement of our conceptualization of global relations. Furthermore, approaches to global political economy should follow such principles, as a recent discussion by John Agnew and Stuart Corbridge (1995) on *Mastering Space* has demonstrated at length: 'the production of space and how it is conceived can be used to convey the sense of how change is occurring. But this is so only if space is historicized; put in a historical context rather than seen as a permanent set of influences or fixed backdrop upon which history is inscribed' (p. x).

Agnew and Corbridge's arguments are prominent in the growing literature on spatiality directly related to the recognition that the 'state-territorial spatial form' simply cannot explain 'all social cleavages' (p. 15; see also Youngs 1998). The critical work on which this study has focused has, in various ways, emphasized that political and economic space contains people, that the conceptualizations and uses of, as well as the meanings attached to, such space are pertinent to understanding power relations. I have considered in depth the distortions inherent in dominant state-centric senses of sovereign being, or sovereign identity, including, importantly, in relation to gender. That discussion has to be taken further in regard to the central concerns of this chapter.

We are returning here to the realist/idealist or utopian opposition and its mobilization and impact in the discipline. The issue to be addressed is the relationship between dominant notions of sovereignty and philosophical and spatial universalisms. As suggested, Walker's (1993) analysis in particular[8] assists in making such connections. It explores sovereignty as a concept that defines political being or identity directly in terms of territorialization or territorial division. The essence of politics is thus located in separation: in the segregation of political units, states or individuals, from one another. Access to the wider world, the universal situation, spatially and philosophically, comes _via_ this ontological as well as methodological, conceptual as well as physical, separation (p. 154). Fundamental interdependence is denied.

Richard Ashley's (1980) early research on political economy directly addressed this issue by integrating knowledge processes into his analysis of security. His approach assists the expansion of agency/structure considerations in identifying knowledge processes as integrated into larger historical processes, as concrete dimensions of the dynamics of history. Thus it concretizes human agency by linking knowledge processes and practices directly to the world in which human beings live and have lived. A critical perspective is produced that both seeks distance from the abstract notions of time and space associated with state-centrism, and affirms the potential for change through human agency on the basis of critical approaches to dominant forms of knowledge.

In his analysis of _The Political Economy of War and Peace_, Ashley (1980) considered the 'security problematique' in global relations in the context of the knowledge processes integral to both the maintenance of existing conditions and their potential for transformation. 'A _problematic_ is defined as an abstracted representation of some aspect of the gap between the actual and preferred human condition' (p. 315). The notion of abstraction is important here, especially for its distinction from the static types of abstraction already identified as intrinsic to state-centric orientations.[9] In Ashley's framework, abstraction indicates the potential for an intellectual/theoretical journey _with_ practical bearing. It concerns the linkage of theory *to* practice, and its aims are contrary to the kinds of conceptual stasis achieved by state-centrism.

The idea of a problematic represents a critical stance: one which, while it may be focused on certain forms of change, recognizes the identifiable influences of history. In other words, while such a stance may represent emancipatory projects, these are always firmly associated with the practical purport of relevant historical processes and structures. Hence Ashley's description of a problematic as 'an anchoring point of departure'. 'Its function is to focus research on the question: How and why did the problematic take form? How and why does it persist? What are the structured processes by which it is reproduced? How and under what conditions might it be transcended?' (p. 315).

Central to the 'security problematique' in contemporary global relations for Ashley is the 'technical-rational logic' driving dominant forms of theory and practice, and, of course, interrelating them (Youngs 1997a). This logic continually presses the principle of ever-expanding human control over the environment,[10] leading to a situation where 'Human knowledge, skills, and capacities to communicate are used, not self-reflectively, but as instrumentalities of problem-solving, control, and domination' (Ashley 1980: 251). According to Ashley's analysis, 'technical-rational logic' confounds the *fundamental* 'interdependence' of humans with one another and with their environment: it objectifies and seeks to control via the application of 'knowledge and skills' and ensures that the *'concepts of autonomy, knowledge, and power are soldered into one'* (pp. 209–16). In this way, the logic can be understood to predetermine questions of agency on its own terms and to work to close off potential for thinking about it otherwise.

Ashley's explanation of the logic demonstrates that interpretations of global relations based on competition, as are common to state-centrism, should be understood in terms not of politics, but of political economy. This logic concerns 'the dynamics of growth, of rivalry, and of balance of power' as steered by problem-solving approaches, which are means–ends orientated and abstracted from time and space to the degree that the terms of 'technical rationality', and the problems themselves, set the prime limits of concern (pp. 210–11). Thus while a continuing adherence to such a logic reflects certain historically produced conditions relating to it, it does not promote a wider critical awareness reaching beyond its own limits either historically or spatially.

Ashley's arguments assert that such logic is 'false' in its conflictual need-producing momentum, but they also recognize that it is 'true' in its relevance to the differentiated situations of human beings in the present era; it is true to the extent that it is 'embedded, layer upon layer, in society's manifest structures and forms' (pp. 214–15). But its ultimate contradiction in representing 'progress toward the destruction of all it has built' (p. 214) impels an alternative logic, which for Ashley is 'rationality proper' and which addresses this contradiction actively through critical awareness of human/human and human/environment 'interdependence' (pp. 215–16). This approach to interdependence treats it as a fundamental consideration, a starting point for analysis, and is distinct from approaches that seek to build considerations of interdependence into analysis which is fundamentally – that is, ontologically and methodologically – individualistic, as is the case with state-centrism.[11]

In essence, 'rationality proper' critiques the abstract tendencies of 'technical rationality' to take account of 'historical-processual influences' on _thought_ as well as action, and asserts the importance of continuing critical thought and the communication and effective sharing of contrasting viewpoints (pp. 216–17).[12] Ashley includes among the positive possibilities for advancement of 'rationality proper' the growth of 'transnational social scientific communities' (pp. 224–8). Two other aspects identified as offering positive potential for 'rationality proper' are issues raised by 'interdependence' and information and communication technologies (pp. 219–24). All three themes are depicted as interlinked, and the general point to note is their emphasis on knowledge and communication on practical and academic levels. They also signal a sense that the positive potential for critical engagement with the dominant influences of 'technical rationality' is to be found in areas most closely associated with its global expansion via industrialization and technologization. Both have contributed to a heightened awareness of interdependence in negative and positive senses, and the involvement of scientists throughout has been intrinsic to the possibility of knowledge claims and their application to practice.

Bearing in mind that Ashley put these arguments forward nearly twenty years ago, they retain some pertinent messages in the light of the growth of interest in globalization, and associated concerns that could broadly be categorized under interdependence understood in the fundamental manner articulated by Ashley (see also Maclean 1984). Most importantly, Ashley's approach builds knowledge into the analytical picture with regard to interdependence, and it does so in a way that associates knowledge with action and thus with questions of agency. It addresses 'technical rationality' as 'a dominant grammar of thought', identifying how its concerns are focused on resulting imperatives and their linkages of human beings to one another and their environment in the broadest senses through 'choices' and action (1980: 175–6). Over time such choices and action contribute to the structural settings within which new 'choices' are made and new action taken. But significantly, Ashley's analysis stresses, this dominant mode of thought is unable to take account of the *full weight of historical circumstances*, at least partly because of its uncritical adherence to the principle of the universal applicability of human control. The tenets of 'technical rationality' as rules of the game become '*interiorized*' in the identities of states and their agents.

> For each state, therefore, opposition to multilateral limits on state autonomy represents an expression of aspects of its deeply structured identity. To the extent that this 'high political' identity pervades and finds expression in all domains of activity – to the extent that it is dominant – states are likely to resist the imposition of multilateral regulative norms, not only in the politico-military domain, but also in the domains of technological, economic, and population growth. (pp. 203–4)

Ashley's consideration of the pervasiveness of 'technical rationality'[13] in political economy presents profound ontological challenges to an understanding of the state. It certainly disrupts arbitrary separations of politics and economics along state and market lines. Perhaps even more fundamentally, it demands that associated knowledge processes are considered internal to the operation of political economy, to its present bases of legitimacy, and to the critical potential for change (see also Murphy and Tooze 1991a).

The critical work in international relations and global political economy considered in this study is directed towards the reclaiming of politics. In my view, it would be misleading to think of them as 'new normative approaches' (Brown 1992), even though they may be considered to include what could be described as varying normative concerns, if the term is understood in its broadest sense. What they seek to do first and foremost is reveal the limited political perspective that realist and neo-realist state-centrism has maintained, to explore its implications in theory and practice, and to introduce contrasting, fuller perspectives, including those sensitive to political economy in radical ways.

Many features entrenched by mainstream state-centrism as assumed foundations have been problematized in the process: the nature of the state; the relationship of time and space to notions of politics and political economy; gendered dimensions of theory and practice; the status of knowledge in social power relations; and oppositional frameworks of understanding, such as national/international, politics/economics, man/woman, subject/object, subjective/objective. The task of investigating global relations has been revealed as even more complex than it was already thought to be; the neat edges of realism's dominant conceptual packages have been profoundly disturbed. No matter how hard those who wish to do so may try, the situation cannot be reversed – that is the conclusion this study seeks to encourage. Examination of the realist/idealist or utopian opposition and its effects provides probably the most convincing explanation of why this is the case, for it reveals the conceptual cage that realism has constructed for itself and within which it is trapped.

Whatever way one looks at it, realist notions of politics are partial in the extreme, reductive and abstract in their rationalistic tendencies. They are concerned with a static worldview, that of predominantly self-interested state-centrism, rather than the dynamics of interaction between differentiated political and economic interests and structural conditions. Too often they presume rather than ponder, assert rather than question. They may negotiate power and politics, they may negotiate change, but along highly delineated conceptual lines. Previous chapters have provided some detailed sense of the static character of realist state-centric politics, and the assessment in this chapter helps to complete the picture.

Mainstream state-centrism predetermines the nature of politics, rather than setting out to discover what it may be in historically contingent circumstances. The motivations of the state-centred disposition are taken as a prime and sufficient explanation of politics. The world is understood predominantly in these terms, which work to exclude normative issues as *real* social forces. The ontological and methodological bases of realist and neorealist framings of politics implicitly and explicitly place normative concerns and influences outside of the realm of *real* – that is, *effective* – politics. Neorealism's collapsing of agency and structure, for example, contributes directly to this reductionism. As Mervyn Frost (1986: 58)[14] has argued with regard to Kenneth Waltz's (1979) approach to structure in *Theory of International Politics*:

> It is clear that Waltz envisages the structure of the international system as being, in some sense, the fundamental determinant of world politics; as being in some way independent of the ideas men happen to have. The international order as a structure of this kind is thus assumed as some kind of basic political 'reality' and it is, moreover, one which clearly diminishes the possible relevance of normative theory.

Frost's discussion, which ranges beyond the scope of realism and neo-realism, highlights the importance of considering normative aspects as inside, rather than outside, politics, and thus, as I have indicated above, as effective rather than ineffective in that context.

> Normative theory always presupposes that actors in the practice of international relations do have alternatives and real choices, and can change their conduct. Only if we accept these presuppositions do ought-statements in the context of international relations make sense. Similarly, normative theory in international relations presupposes that the international order itself can be deliberately changed in specified ways. In short, then, normative theory presupposes that there is an important sense in which people's normative ideas can shape the order in which they live. (pp. 54–5)

For Frost (pp. 64, 71), 'a state is not a political reality which exists independently of the ideas (including normative ones) which people adhere to', and account should be taken of the extent to which power is 'based on co-operation according to norms'. Normative issues should thus be considered internal, not external, to politics – to political reality – and the failings of realist and neorealist state-centred perspectives cannot be underestimated on this score.

Furthermore, as this study has sought to illustrate, considerations of globalization and globalizing processes draw attention to the degree to which such questions should be addressed with close regard to issues of spatiality, indeed to the political economy of spatiality, as will be explored in part III. Previous chapters have set out the extreme nature of spatial assumptions in dominant state-centric approaches to international relations. It has been explained that they work against the development of dynamic perspectives on political economy through the ontological and causal primacy they allocate to the realm of politics. This chapter seeks to increase understanding of linkages between the resulting reductionism of global analysis *and* conceptualizations of spatiality.

It is important to emphasize that state-centrism's reduction of politics inherently implies a reductive sense of global space. Its determinism interrelates the spatial and human via the state-centred ontological prism. What we see when we look through this prism is a chain of politics that links states to states, and implicitly within them and *via* them, as Walker has stressed, humans to humans. Global space is, in profound senses, an empty category in relation to this state-centric framework of analysis. If it can be considered to exist at all in any meaningful way, it is only as the spatial *other* to the bounded political unit of the state. It is merely what lies beyond. And, as discussed above, state-centred notions of politics, in being territorially defined, link interests and values to specifically articulated notions of space. It is not just the physical world of global space that can be accessed only via state-centred politics; it is also the philosophical realm of global human concerns, however these might be defined.

The point here is not to underestimate the importance of states and their influence in global politics, but to stress the ontological limitations that state-centred conceptualizations place on one's capacities to assess that influence accurately and, perhaps most importantly, dynamically, as part of the endeavour to analyse global relations more comprehensively. This study will consider further the degree to which states are not separate from, but are intrinsic to, global changes of many kinds, notably those which relate, and are changing the relationship between, politics and economics. Such developments deeply problematize assumed separations between the inside and outside of states, between politics and economics, with direct implications for spatial questions. Spatiality has been underconceptualized in the study of both international relations and international political economy.

New analytical contexts for normative concerns

The critiques assessed in this book have made key contributions to the possibilities for deeper spatial sensitivity among analysts in these areas. It is partly for this reason that I have suggested they should be regarded as reclaiming politics rather than as 'new normative approaches'. The distinction is more important than at first it might seem. These critiques, far from representing another stage in the normative school of thought, have sought to create quite new analytical contexts for considering normative concerns. They have, in a range of ways, directly attacked the realist/idealist or utopian dualism, and actively worked to overcome the reductionist vision of politics that state-centred realist tendencies have imposed through their dominance based on this oppositional framework. They have done so by refusing to treat states as abstract territorially defined units, and by arguing, on a variety of grounds, that they are political and economic spaces, characterized by practices that are related to questions of authority, legitimacy and identity.[15] Regard should be paid here to how much they have contributed to a reformulation of the understanding of politics and political economy, in stark contrast to the reductionist notion of these categories common to dominant state-centrism. The basis of this reformulation is a refusal to treat politics or political economy as static or abstract, and a determination to ground them, literally: treating them as processes involving people operating within territorially defined and spatially structured circumstances, as articulated by discursive as well as more obviously material practices associated with power relations.[16]

There are a number of points to make here about the implications of this opening out, this expansion of understanding of processes of

politics and political economy. Spatial issues are central to the challenge
that this development represents to the entrenched 'levels of analysis',
vertically hierarchical perspective that state-centrism has played so
substantial a role in perpetuating. The critiques I have looked at are
seeking, in varying ways, to provide quite a different spatial sense of
global relations, one that is multidimensional and that contextualizes
power relations in time and space, albeit from differing theoretical perspectives. Ashley's and Walker's considerations, and those of the forms
of gender analysis examined, uncover the deeper social aspects of territoriality. Differentiation through social structures and practices, including those considered to be discursive, has been identified as fundamental
to an understanding of power as process, and thus of politics and political economy as process. Questions of overturning abstract approaches
to humanity, to individuality, have explicitly and implicitly been revealed through these discussions as vital to such endeavours.

The extreme partiality of the rational-man-writ-large, dominant
state-centric approach has been demonstrated ontologically and methodologically. Its eradication of complex considerations of agency is
directly associated with the high level of abstraction it allocates to its
key actor, its prime political unit, the state. But, as has been increasingly
suggested in this study, its limitations in considering even that unit as
an agent in any form of dynamic agent/structure context are substantial. Neorealism's ultimate conflation of actor, agency and structure is a
determining factor here. It may seem a rather simple statement to claim
that the critical approaches referred to above have attacked this abstract
and static stance towards global relations by, among other things, putting
people back into the picture, but it signals a range of serious ontological
and methodological, as well as epistemological, issues.

Epistemology has been one of the major underlying themes of this
book: its orientation has included a recognition that assessments of what
counts as knowledge are directly relevant to the conceptual challenge of
enhancing the approach to global relations. Briefly, it is a form of analysis that seeks to problematize knowledge forms and what they say about
the world, and to implicate them in considerations of power relations
and thus of the difficult areas of structure and agency. The purpose has
been not to produce new theories but to undertake what might be label-
led critical conceptual groundwork. The aim has been to reveal the bases
for, and nature of, conceptual parameters of dominant state-centric
traditions, and to demonstrate how recent critical work facilitates escape
from them. Take, for example, the apparently simple notion of people
being put into the picture. The intention here is to make analysis of
global relations *concrete* rather than *abstract* in terms of human beings,

while at the same time taking into account the problematics generated by universalistic approaches to notions of _human_. This is not, it turns out, simple at all, because it introduces inescapable ontological, episte-mological and methodological challenges, notably to understanding of power, with which mainstream state-centric adherents claim to be primarily concerned. I shall consider this area further in the discussion of hegemony, a concept that frames the _international_ orientation of these mainstream perspectives on power.

I have argued that state-centric perspectives are based on a concept-ualization of the state as a reductive and essentially empty category. An important aspect of the contributions of the kinds of critical work discussed here has been to fill up that category, to explore its political and economic content, and to address different dimensions of its social relations of power, including those associated with gender. As a result, the state is no longer an abstraction; it becomes a dynamic social reality. Naturally, what seems to be the conceptual clarity and power of the ab-stract state-centric framework is lost. Everything looks much less clearly defined – it all begs explanation. Without the neat assumptions that domi-nant state-centrism embraces, questions continue to be opened up: noth-ing is settled; in fact, quite the reverse – conceptually much is disturbed. But this is the unsurprising result of the breaking of state-centrism's conceptual bonds. It is largely why it can be argued that this critical development is better understood as a reclaiming of politics, and to some degree of political economy, than as a new normative stage.

For all their many differences, including fundamental theoretical ones, the critical approaches discussed in this book share an important qual-ity: the drive for new non-state-centric forms of comprehending power in global relations. In straightforward senses, they have in varying ways removed the state from its abstracted role in understanding of those relations, and placed it actively and firmly back within them. This has had implications for thinking about theory as a form of practice and its relationships to wider realms of practice. These are revolutionary pressures not least for their incorporation of epistemological, as well as ontological and methodological, aspects – revolutionary in their multiplicitous attempts, some indirect as well as direct, to break apart the state-centric prism in ways that are as vital to understanding the changes affecting states themselves as to investigating global relations in a non-state-centric fashion. These attempts prompt one to abandon the assumptions of state-centrism in favour of investigations that in-clude interest in the changing nature of states and their power, particu-larly in the context of the global political economy.

The writings of Ashley and Walker have been noted for, among other things, the extent to which they open up an understanding of the state as political process: in other words, for offering conceptual access to the state as a dynamic social entity. This enables a view of states as implicated in, rather than abstracted from, processes of inclusion and exclusion, of social territorialization.[17] Mainstream state-centrism's starting point of the state as discrete political unit has buried such issues under its central assumptions. Numerous questions associated with considerations of globalization, including, for example, migration, citizenship and democracy, require their exposure.[18] What is more, this exposure problematizes the state as the category or political unit through which human beings should be understood to access the wider world, including other human beings. Territorially *and* philosophically, the state, in this respect, can be understood to have played a prime role, in theory and practice, in expressing *separateness*.[19] The realist/idealist or utopian opposition entrenches this notion of separateness through its partial view of state-centred politics. What is communicated by the forms of critical analysis considered in this study is that we need perspectives on politics and political economy that are much less reductive than those of dominant traditions of realism or neorealism.

The discussion in this chapter prompts consideration of how normative questions relate to such developments. It is clear that theory should reflect the fact that such questions are internal rather than external to politics and political economy. Even in areas of social relations where normative concerns are minimized, including through structural influences over time, this remains a matter of politics, of political economy. The supra-rationality of mainstream realist and neorealist standpoints counters such understanding, removes it from active consideration. The reclaiming of politics and political economy therefore includes the imperative to address how to negotiate the normative in a new and integrated fashion in analysis. This is a difficult area and there is not space here to examine it in detail. Only a few points directly relevant to the concerns of this study can be made.

At the beginning of this chapter, I recalled the historical roots of the realist/idealist split in international relations theorizing. Half a century later, realism's preoccupations with security and sovereignty in the interests of international order have a distinct pertinence when placed in historical context (Fukuyama 1992: 245–53). The static orientation of realism that has come so strongly under fire in this study must have looked very different at a time of devastating human upheaval in the wake of the unprecedented scale of international conflict in World War Two. The drive towards stability and the imperative for a *realistic* approach to ensuring that it lasted were characteristics of that time that are hard to capture now. However, a major question that can be posed is: how well has realism served us?

This study's viewpoint is clearly negative in this respect, and this is not to suggest that realism and neorealism do not reveal important dimensions of global relations. The critical focus adopted here has been deliberately centred on their specific forms of state-centrism and the implications of these. It has been indicated that these are serious and profound in ontological, epistemological and methodological terms: that is, in what they regard as the essence of global relations, in their bases for gaining knowledge about those relations, and in the methods used to do so. For example, the distortions of state-centrism have led to partial attention to the full roles of major organizations such as the United Nations and the European Union, which have been formed _by_ states. The _high politics_ orientation of mainstream state-centrism has led to a concentration of interest on the foreign policy and security roles of such organizations, with assessment of their wider relevance generally left to specialists in the area of international organizations. Social, technical and humanitarian issues, in which UN agencies have had significant involvement, as well as broader questions of political economy connected with the EU, are dim spots in the distance when global relations are regarded through the state-centric prism. These are areas relevant to a reclaiming of politics and political economy as discussed above, because, undoubtedly, normative questions are more strongly identified with such _low politics_ concerns, particularly those denoted as humanitarian and social, and much less strongly identified with the high politics concerns upon which mainstream state-centric approaches have concentrated.

This also illustrates why a rejection of conceptualizations of politics and political economy as rationalistic abstractions, and moves toward recognizing them as processes involving people and thus social relations of power in their fullest sense, are so important. The scope and the impact of entities such as the UN and EU are global in many regards and directly contribute to the structural conditions and daily circumstances of billions of people. In these times of apparently endemic global recessionary pressures, it would be absurd to regard the EU – which with the USA and Japan is generally regarded as forming the triad of power in the global economy[20] – as an influence external to state security concerns, especially those of its members, and especially those related to economic security, on a global as well as a regional scale. Such complexities of the global political economy compel a move beyond simplistic state-mediated perspectives and the territorial limitations that they impose on our understanding.[21] Sovereignty as an encapsulation of the identity of the state and its power is a key concept in this respect. Saskia Sassen (1996: 28–9) talks in terms of an 'unbundling of sovereignty', arguing that 'sovereignty has been decentred and territory partly denationalized'.

For a range of reasons, it is far from satisfactory to *assume* human experience as solely or even primarily mediated by states. Globalizing processes have increasingly made this a problematic area and it should be treated as such. What this means is that the central assumptions of state-centrism as set out in this and previous chapters should be swept away. This is particularly important in relation to notions of territoriality and boundaries, which are central to understanding the social relations of power. They cannot be assumed; they need to be investigated. Inevitably, as this study has shown, this draws us into questions of identity, including gendered identity, and associated questions of knowledge and power. It also draws us into general issues of inclusion and exclusion, political, economic and cultural (Walker 1993: 159–83).

This discussion has highlighted ways in which dominant state-centric forms of knowledge can be considered directly implicated in such processes. Discursive practices are just that: part of practice, even when they claim the status of theory. Thus they are political in the broadest sense of that term – they are about power. Walker's (1993) critical examination of sovereignty is a cogent demonstration of this point, a powerful reminder that the assumptions that have become buried in concepts over time should not be forgotten. After reading his challenging arguments at length, one is left with a deep impression of how many considerations have been outlawed by the realist state-centric framework's capacity to hijack the ideal ground through the particularistic assertion of the primacy of 'inside' over 'outside'. Walker's analysis signals the degree to which it is both the immediacy of people's lives and grander notions of wider connections between them that such perspectives inhibit – the local as well as the global.

> The character of the community in which people actually live, work, love and play together has seemed unproblematic and uninteresting, of peripheral importance to the serious business of capital and state. To engage with the local is to be side-tracked into the trivial; to aspire to some broader and more universal conception of humanity is to recede into the mists of utopia. It is not possible to be 'realistic' or 'practical' or 'relevant' in such places. (pp. 152–3)

This kind of critique affirms the breadth of epistemological concerns confronting those wishing to enhance conceptualizations of global relations. In straightforward respects, there is a multifaceted struggle to revolutionize what are considered legitimate forms of knowledge in the study of international relations and global political economy.

The most fundamental challenge comes from gender critiques, which insist that the gendered nature of politics and political economy be recognized as essential to understanding power. These critiques have maintained an extremely strong theory/practice purchase, but it is important to note the extent to which they have sought new ground, both in theory and in practice. Christine Sylvester's introductory comments to a special issue of *Alternatives* (1993) entitled 'Feminists Write International Relations' are notable in this context:

> the reader will find almost no talk in these pages of how international relations should be defined and differentiated from other terrains of politics. How insubordinate to virtually ignore 'the field'. It is as though these writers have seen little point in delineating 'a' feminist international relations in a world where boundaries blur in ways that deny women agency at home and at large. Customs of scholarship routinely absent people called women from most realms of politics, as though everywhere we were latter-day Botticelli Venuses nakedly oblivious to the morass around us. When we do enter international relations, we are strange visitors to be monitored – Amazon warriors, sneaks, smugglers, and prostitutes in the world, veiled fundamentalists. In not-defining international relations, it is clear that these feminist writers refuse to save or caretake a women-eclipsing field. Their point is to spotlight the situations and struggles that transgress assigned lands of scholarship, identity, and practice. (p. 2)

These statements carry many messages, the strongest being against the partialities of male-centred analysis. Their tone is a fitting close to this chapter's outline of the political nature of territorialization, including in theoretical terms. Part of its main purpose has been to consider linkages between philosophical and spatial boundaries, to facilitate understanding of theory as a dynamic part of social relations of power. Developing capacities to analyse these relations in global contexts incorporates theory as practice and the critical imperatives produced by such a move.

Conclusion

This part of the book has examined key aspects of the structure of theoretical exchange which have contributed to the perpetuation of dominant state-centrism's conceptual determinism. It has explored in greater detail the critical challenges that undermine this situation and provide the bases for moving beyond reductionist state-centric parameters.

Particularistic forms of paradigmatism and the normative divide have been identified as the major areas of concern. In the case of the former, I have explained that superficial paradigmatism has veiled the fundamental paradigmatism of state-centrism. Furthermore, and of equal concern to this study, enduring paradigmatism even in the context of 'the third debate', which actually addresses power/knowledge/discourse issues, has retained a patriarchally oriented hierarchy of thought, leaving the deep insights of gender critiques to one side. The assessment of paradigmatism has demonstrated the profound and enduring *barriers* to meaningful and effective debate in international relations and international political economy even, crucially, in what would generally be regarded as their most critical branches of thought.

My consideration of the normative divide takes the general point about barriers to meaningful and effective debate further, linking it directly to state-centrism's highly partial approach to politics and the persistent role of the realist/idealist dualism in legitimizing this partiality. Calling on the critical concerns that are the main focus of this book, I have outlined how a more realistic approach to politics, and indeed political economy, is called for on many fronts, an approach that treats so-called normative questions associated with values and interests, including those related to knowledge practices, as internal rather than external to politics. Further illustrations have been provided of the ways in which the critical perspectives examined in this study help us understand both this point and the bases for moving forward in relation to it. This discussion has also expanded consideration of the ties that bind reductive approaches to politics to reductive approaches to spatiality through the state-centric prism. Fixed interpretations of politics, time and space are at issue here. The focus of part III is on dynamic alternatives relating to political economy and spatiality.

Part III

The Spaces of Global Relations

Part III develops the critical points raised in parts I and II about state-centrism's assumptions and its static and reductive approach to politics and political identity. Focus is placed on the bases for approaches to time and space that break through state-centrism's sovereign boundaries and reflect the changing nature of both states themselves and the wider world political economy. I argue that, in different ways, the critical approaches discussed in parts I and II signal the need for a more complex sense of spatiality, one not based on assumed separations between state and market, politics and economics, but one seeking to assess changes in their interrelationships with regard to spatial and temporal contexts. Intrinsic to such a sense of spatiality is a recognition of social dynamics, that politics and political economy are about people, that they concern social relations of power. Chapter 5 opens up consideration of a political economy of spatiality approach and examines how this enhances the conceptualization of global relations.

The starting point for the first section of this chapter is that the dominance of state-centric perspectives has contributed substantially to a lack of attention to spatiality. Abstract notions of states and markets, politics and economics, as outlined in parts I and II, have basically left spatial consideration to one side. Thinking globally, I explain, has increasingly come to be understood as thinking spatially, but this does not mean thinking about global space as some kind of homogeneous, undifferentiated mass. Thinking spatially means taking spatial dimensions of social relations seriously. Territory, which has been too empty a category in the study of international relations, reduced via state-centrism to its qualities of boundedness, requires open consideration, including in relation to the state. I return to John Herz's work on territoriality as an illustration of the early signs of this necessity raised by the nuclear issue and its profound challenges to the container notion of the state in that most fundamental area of the concerns of international relations: security.

Neorealist approaches to hegemony and their expanded attention to political economy in this context are starkly contrasted with Gramscian frameworks. In the former, I argue, the state-centric assumptions and lack of regard for spatiality endure. That political economy occurs in spatial contexts is too much taken for granted, as is the nature of those contexts themselves. In the latter, on the contrary, there are efforts to open up time/space questions as part of understanding the dynamics of political economy. The next section of chapter 5 discusses how this contributes to the reclaiming and reinventing of agency. I explain how Gramscian standpoints, rather than conflating agency and structure in the manner of neorealism, seek to explore their dynamics. This discussion is broadened to incorporate questions of identity in the context of the breadth of critical approaches assessed in the study, including those concentrating on gender and public/private considerations.

The final section of the chapter explores how such considerations radicalize spatial understanding of the local in relation to global/local linkages commonly identified as central to assessments of processes of globalization. Gendered perspectives prioritize the public/private issue in this respect, demanding that domestic space be taken seriously in ways that mainstream analysis has never done. This also entails taking feminist reinterpretations of agency seriously, including with regard to the personal as political. Such reinterpretations are distant from the abstractions of the rational-man-writ-large notions of state-centrism and its male-centred assumptions. Gendered sensitivities to public/private dynamics in social relations recognize that dominant patterns of socialized and institutionalized gendered behaviour centrally involve physical aspects of identity. Sexual relations, child-bearing and rearing, the role of caring, and gendered notions of physicality are among the considerations here. I discuss how gendered dimensions of power are deeply embedded in political economy, as evidenced in the high degree of differentiation in the structure of, and rewards – or lack of them – for, contrasting productive functions and their definitions in society.

Chapter 6 outlines in more detail the major concerns of a political economy of spatiality approach. These include the rethinking of social boundaries. The state remains a key category, but it is not an assumed state in the mode of state-centrism's conceptual determinism. Focus is placed rather on state/market interactions and their relevance to boundary transformations. Saskia Sassen's work on the 'decentred' nature of contemporary sovereignty is discussed for its capacities to increase our awareness of the changing qualities of states. Foucaultian perspectives on governmentality focusing on the citizen or subject/government relationship are also identified as probing states as process. In the next section in the chapter, on inequality and spatiality, emphasis is placed on concerns with states as disaggregated social entities. In examining the United Nations _Human Development Report_, I highlight the trends of economic polarization it details, within as well as between countries. In various ways, concentrations of wealth and power, including, for example, in global cities, cannot be understood, I argue, within the spatial confines of state-centric perspectives.

This section of the chapter discusses the role of consumption as well as production in assessments of inequality, and the importance of economic as well as political subjects, and thus of issues of identity in economic as well as political terms. Here I consider Scott Lash and John Urry's work on 'economies of signs and space' as indicative of the kind of complexities that the contemporary global political economy presents for understanding subjects and subjectivity. Their delineating of inequality on social and spatial bases, and to some extent on the basis of relative time/space freedoms or restrictions, is highlighted.

The final section of chapter 6 focuses on space/time relations and patriarchal structures. I argue that the household colonization of private – that is, domestic – female time has yet to be taken into full account. The expanding age of the double burden for women, in which they must work both inside and outside the home, highlights the growing importance of this situation. Drawing on a number of examples, I illustrate how the dynamics of globalization should be regarded as, among other things, a dynamics of patriarchal forces, only some of which are geographically and historically indigenous. The interaction of these forces in particular places and at particular times reveals some of the deepest aspects of the dynamics of inequality in globalization. I argue that this is a key way to probe the inner dimensions of globalization and demonstrate why this is the case.

5 | States, Time and Space

With the state-centric blinkers removed, what do we see? This is the major question addressed by this and the following chapter. It is clearly a vast topic and only a few aspects of it can be covered. These will be selected on the basis of their links to the earlier considerations of this study. The reasons for this are not restricted to consistency. The discussion that follows considers a range of perspectives related to the broad area of globalization, but it seeks to do so in a manner highlighting shared conceptual challenges and analytical interests across the disciplinary areas involved, including international relations and global political economy. One of the most striking characteristics of new forms of global study is their multidisciplinarity (see, for example, Featherstone, Lash and Robertson 1995). This opens up exciting new possibilities for understanding, but it also presents dangers of confusion in the bases upon which such understanding may be built. To some extent such dangers are unavoidable, but we can seek to address them where possible. Intellectual *borrowings* are bound to occur in such circumstances for the very best of reasons, and this study itself demonstrates such tendencies. But the greater the awareness of the deeper circumstances within which such borrowings take place, the better.

The arguments in this volume seek to contribute to such awareness in considering the conceptual limitations of realist and neorealist state-centrism and ways in which the structure of theoretical debate has contributed to their influence. I have emphasized that recent preoccupations with globalizing processes have, if anything, heightened interest in the state and changes affecting its political and economic characteristics, roles and influences (see, in particular, Sassen 1996). In many ways, the status of the state as a social force is being rethought in relation to a range of globalizing pressures: political, economic and cultural (see, for example, McGrew, Lewis et al. 1992; Featherstone 1990). The identities of states in these regards are viewed as undergoing profound change, including in relation to their citizens, whose participation in the global political economy can be less and less easily understood in state-centred terms (Youngs 1997b, 1997c).

Patterns of authority and accountability affecting citizens need to be mapped increasingly on transnational bases with attention paid to international institutions, including powerful corporations but also key policy groups such as the G7 – a kind of global economic *cabinet* of major western economies – whose activities and decisions are distanced from the democratic processes of even member states, let alone the larger group of non-member states whose economies are also influenced. Saskia Sassen (1996: 32) has clarified that 'Together with sovereignty and exclusive territoriality, citizenship marks the specificity of the modern state.' She has rightly identified 'economic citizenship' as 'a strategic research site', arguing that 'The institution and construct of citizenship are being destabilized.' She explores the notion of economic citizenship residing in firms and markets, especially global financial markets, rather than in individual citizens (pp. 34–58). In common with complex multidisciplinary debates about 'cosmopolitan democracy', her investigations focus on the problematics of individual citizenship remaining an *effective* and *meaningful*, but certainly *transformed*, category in post-state-centred times.

For analysts like David Held (1995), 'cosmopolitan democracy' represents a detailed reformulation of democratic structures and processes to take account of contemporary transnational conditions. In simple terms, such an approach posits the possibility of an internationalization of democracy, including through laws and institutions, some of which, such as the United Nations and European Union, already exist but would require adaptation. Rethinking the *inter-national* is characteristic of recent work associated with sovereignty, citizenship and democracy. Critical spatial perspectives on the state as category, as political and economic container, are evident in such work in varying degrees, explicitly or implicitly.

Earlier chapters have highlighted three results of dominant state-centrism that are conceptual barriers in this respect. The first is a deterministic state-centric approach to spatial conceptualization; the second is a static orientation towards the state, a failure to treat it as a dynamic social entity; the third is a fixed abstraction of the time/space relationship through the concept of sovereignty. The struggle of the critical approaches upon which I have concentrated has focused strongly on these three associated areas. They have, in different ways, signalled the need for a more complex sense of spatiality, one not based on assumed separations between state and market, politics and economics, but one seeking to assess the changes in their interrelationships with regard to spatial and temporal contexts. Intrinsic to such a sense of spatiality is a recognition of social dynamics, that politics and political economy are about people, that they concern social relations of power. This is one of the most problematic imperatives in a field where dominant forms of state-centrism have produced reductive approaches to politics, asserted the primacy of politics over economics, and effaced agency/structure sensitivities through abstract frameworks.

The previous chapter stressed the priority of putting people back into the picture. This chapter explores why that is central to a political economy of spatiality approach, and how this approach assists the enhancement of the conceptualization of global relations. Its intention is to provide conceptual signposts for future directions in thinking about global relations. These are associated with both the critical directions set out so far in this study and wider multidisciplinary concerns with new approaches to _the global_ rather than _the inter-national_. State-centred approaches have given international relationists a particular purchase on the inter-national, but have resulted in conceptual limitations that are extreme when thinking in wider terms of the global. New and open approaches to spatiality are central in this respect.

Spatiality

If one category has traditionally been least conceptualized in the study of international relations and global political economy, it is spatiality. The dominance of state-centric perspectives has contributed substantially to this situation. Abstract notions of states and markets, politics and economics, have basically left spatial consideration to one side. Thinking globally, however, has increasingly come to be understood as thinking spatially (Harvey 1990; Lash and Urry 1994; Demko and Wood 1994). This does not mean, of course, that _global space_ can be considered as some kind of homogeneous, undifferentiated mass; quite the reverse. To think spatially is to take spatial dimensions of social relations seriously, to recognize that political, economic and cultural exchanges take place in different forms of social space and, together with structural influences, contribute to how that space is framed and perceived. Space is not just a blank backdrop to human relations; it is socially constituted, and must therefore be regarded as a contingent element of the dynamics of social relations, and directly relevant to considerations of agency/structure issues.

Mastering Space, the title of an important new work by John Agnew and Stuart Corbridge (1995), has particular meanings in the traditions of international relations. State-to-state conflict and the importance of territory in war and conquest have been prime concerns of the discipline. Major focal points this century, the two world wars, the cold war and its demise, and the subsequent extended conflict in former Yugoslavia, have all highlighted the enduring importance of territorial control in international affairs. Imperialism and post-imperialism have demonstrated for centuries that such control is as much about political economy and culture[1] as it is about the so-called *high politics* of foreign affairs, and that attention to power and human costs should cover all these areas. But territory has predominantly been too empty a category, little more than a political definition of space.[2] Dominant state-centrism has taken it too much for granted as an element of power, and has tended conceptually to leave it barren in terms of social dynamics. This is now as pressing a problem for understanding the state as it is for gaining a fuller comprehension of global relations.

Aspects of the early debate about the 'rise and demise of the territorial state' (Herz 1957) gave early indications of this imperative. Perhaps this is because it related directly to the most profound global risk that has yet to confront humanity, that of nuclear destruction. With international relations' firm focus on security as a prime concern and the identified role of states as guardians of security, the question of nuclear reach was destabilizing. What is interesting about John Herz's (1957) early discussion of this topic is the manner in which he argued that the nuclear age highlighted not the abstract idea of the state, but the concrete territoriality of it.

> What is it that ultimately accounted for the peculiar unity, compactness, coherence of the modern nation-state, setting it off from other nation-states as a separate, independent, and sovereign power? It would seem that this underlying factor is to be found neither in the sphere of law nor in that of politics, but rather in that substratum of statehood where the state unit confronts us, as it were, in its physical, corporeal capacity: as an expanse of territory encircled for its identification and its defense by a 'hard shell' of fortifications. (p. 474)

At issue here, in Herz's words, was the 'impenetrability' or 'territoriality' of the modern state, which was now threatened by the existence of nuclear weaponry. This undermined its basic security role – a situation that could be regarded as paradoxical in Herz's view, for while it signalled the rise of state power, it also ensured its 'vulnerability' as a political unit. It was the global reach of nuclear destructive potential that concerned Herz: 'Since we are inhabitants of a planet of limited (and, as it now seems, insufficient) size, we have reached the limit within which the effect of the means of destruction has become absolute' (p. 489). He anticipated the time when multiple powers would possess nuclear capability and summed up the 'security dilemma' (as pertinent today as in the 1950s) thus: 'Since thermonuclear war would in all likelihood involve one's own destruction together with the opponent's, the means through which the end would have to be attained defeats the end itself. Pursuance of the "logical" security objective would result in mutual annihilation rather than in one unit's global control of a pacified world' (p. 492).

For Herz, this situation challenged fundamentally the concepts of 'sovereignty' and 'absolute power' associated with state-centred views of international relations, and provided a new rationale for security solutions at the global level. Later, Herz (1968) expressed a less pessimistic approach, allowing that some stability could arise from 'mutual deterrence', but this does not detract from the force of his insights on the changing 'territorial' character of the state as a political unit with regard to its role as guarantor of security for its citizens.[3] He also commented on the increasing role of 'informal penetration' (Scott 1962) via 'new technological penetrabilities' (Herz 1968: 26), allowing such activities as 'observation and collection of information from space satellites and through telephotography'.

Such early discussions of challenges to state-centrism's conceptual parameters need to be recalled because of their firm attachment to the territorial nature of the state and the changing political meanings which could be attached to that territoriality and the security associated with it. Furthermore, Herz's direct concern with the impact on the key state-centred concepts of sovereignty and power has resonance with recent critiques of state-centrism discussed in this study. His notion of 'the passing of the age of territoriality' (Herz 1957: 475) is pertinent to current discussions about globalization. It is not surprising that such an early awareness of the problematics of state-centred thinking in international relations should be prompted by the altered security environment produced by nuclear weaponry. As Herz stressed, security, the state and territorial integrity had previously been regarded as synonymous in a way that they never could be again. These changed conditions tested the very nature of the state as 'the basic political unit' (p. 474). The general implication was that the state's claim to political authority had been tied directly to its capacities to protect those within its territory, and that this claim could no longer be maintained in the same form that it had in the past.

It could be argued that this 'security dilemma' affecting the political status of the state has remained unresolved, and continues as a basic element of the changing relationship between state and citizen, in theory and practice, which is relevant to contemporary discussions of globalization and the multiplication of 'risk' factors in contemporary life (Beck 1992; Giddens 1991b, 1994; Lash and Urry 1994). In some respects, this basic 'security dilemma' and mainstream international relations' concerns with it have been in danger of being overlooked in these discussions. It is interesting to note how low a profile it has in a recent important collection on 'geopolitical perspectives' (Demko and Wood 1994), which reflects the broadening of the debate to cover 'resources, the environment, and population', and areas such as information and communication, but fails to place any great focus on old-fashioned security issues.

While the meanings of security have expanded in a globalized world, we would do well to remember the fundamental and prime role played by the nuclear era. I am struck by the enduring relevance of aspects of Herz's assessment of the 'rise and demise of the territorial state'. Its clarification of the linkages between the state's political status and its capacities to secure those within a bounded territory provides, in its own terms, just as useful a critical framework for thinking about global relations now as it did forty years ago.

Herz's arguments provided early grounds for recognizing that spatiality should not be reduced to state-bounded definitions of territory. The points covered in this study promote a much more open interest in spatiality and the interactions between political, economic and cultural influences within it. The next chapter will touch on cultural concerns, but the points to be set out now, establishing the importance of an integrated conceptual attitude to political economy – that is, one which emphasizes the crossflow between political and economic dimensions and spatiality – provide a basis for that discussion. Spatial definitions are intrinsic to power relations. They are asserted structurally over time through institutions and institutional forces such as dominant ideas, attitudes and practices, and they are essential to considerations of agency and the challenges that form part of its processes, as will be explored further below.

The whole question of defining space – the capacity to do it, who does it, how it is done and the differentiated impacts – is fundamental to understanding power. Too little attention has been paid to this issue at the most basic levels in the study of international relations. The politics of maps is an underdeveloped concern that deserves much greater attention, and itself provides an introductory sensitivity to the kinds of topic under examination here (Henrikson 1994). Maps present reality in particular ways – the most common awareness of this has come with the contrast of Pacific-centred and Atlantic-centred representations of the world. But the matter goes much deeper than that. Perspectives on geopolitics explicitly and implicitly address questions of spatiality (Dalby 1996; Parker 1996; Cohen 1994). Hegemony is, among other things, power exercised spatially, thus theories of hegemony should embrace this consideration. The state-centric tradition, and its reductionist impact as assessed in this study, have ensured that this is all too seldom the case. This is one of the central critical thrusts of Agnew and Corbridge's (1995) thesis on hegemony, which emphasizes geopolitics as essential to understanding the key concept of _order_. In their discussion of 'the concept of geopolitical order' they argue:

> Orders necessarily have geographical characteristics. These include the relative degree of centrality of state territoriality to social and economic activities, the nature of the hierarchy of states (dominated by one or a number of states, the degree of state equality), the spatial scope of the activities of different states and other actors such as international organizations and businesses, the spatial connectedness or disconnectedness between various actors, the conditioning effects of informational and military technologies upon spatial interaction, and the ranking of world regions and particular states by the dominant states in terms of 'threats' to their military and economic 'security'. (p. 15)

Neorealism has produced a wealth of work[4] in the area of hegemony and there is no doubt that this has expanded mainstream attention to issues of political economy. But it has little regard for spatiality as the concept is presented here. The standard realist conceptualization of the state as an empty category in this regard, an abstract political unit, is largely to blame for this shortcoming. That political economy occurs in spatial contexts is too much taken for granted, as is the nature of those contexts themselves. These issues are just not explored; neorealist ontology does not require it. One might have hoped that the conceptualization of international regimes (Krasner 1983) as, broadly speaking, shared frameworks for action would have prompted a rethinking of spatial questions, but it has fundamentally retained abstract approaches to politics and economics in this respect. Regime analysis, with its broader interest in institutional influence internationally, should have raised critical awareness of spatiality, but the ontological assumptions of state-centrism were undoubtedly a potent force against such a possibility.

This situation has also affected the growing concentration on governance as a way of confronting 'order and change in world politics'

(Rosenau and Czempiel 1992). This new focus is important both for its attention to the shifts in the location of authority from governments to 'centralizing and decentralizing dynamics', and for its basic assertion that 'governance is not synonymous with government' (J. N. Rosenau 1992: 3–4).[5] Indeed, it is one of the areas with most potential for a new sensitivity to spatiality, but this has been slow to arrive in any overt and developed sense. I would argue that this is largely due to an insufficient regard for the critiques of mainstream state-centric ontology and its enduring explicit and implicit influence. This impacts severely on conceptualization of change, which has always been problematic in the field.[6]

The essentially static nature of state-centric ontology is in extreme tension with efforts to negotiate international or global change; that much should be clear from the above discussions. Embedded within the conceptual architecture of state-centrism is too strong a preoccupation with an essentialized and timeless worldview of *anarchic state-centred order*. This has always hindered adequate conceptualization or theorization of change in mainstream thinking, but this limitation has come to matter even more in the context of new foci, such as governance, which are directly concerned with aspects of global change. It is not possible simply to move on to such analysis without addressing the ontological assumptions built into dominant ideas of order, which, as Rob Walker (1993) has argued, fix time and space in a particularized relationship through the key concept of sovereignty (see also Camilleri and Falk 1992: 221–32).

Assessment of global change relates to *both* time and space and, vitally, the relationship between them (Harvey 1990; Giddens 1991b), so it is evident that a critical and interactive sensitivity to both temporality and spatiality is required. The impact of dominant patterns of state-centric thinking continues to impede such conceptual developments, and the points set out above are aimed at increasing awareness of why this is the case. A major factor is the entrenchment of abstract and static state-centric orientations in structural realism, or neorealism as it is better known. Structural analysis is intended to provide a historical perspective on power, but neorealism's articulation of structure is intrinsically undynamic and its anarchic and rationalistic principles offer an unchanging worldview. In this respect, neorealist perspectives on hegemony are as insensitive to time as they are to space. They assume a state-centred world history at an ontological level. Their consideration of change derives from this position rather than critically interrogating it at any depth.

Gramscian critiques have made a significant contribution to opening up time/space questions within the field, not least owing to their attention to the dynamics of political economy, which contrasts sharply with mainstream state-centrism's deterministic hierarchy of politics over economics.

> Political economy ... is concerned with the historically constituted frameworks or structures within which political and economic activity takes place. It stands back from the apparent fixity of the present to ask how the existing structures came into being and how they may be changing, or how they may be induced to change. In this sense, political economy is critical theory. (Cox 1995: 32)

Robert Cox's (1981) 'social forces, states and world orders' perspective on hegemony, which sought to integrate 'material capabilities, ideas and institutions' in assessing power and change, is indicative of the kinds of sensitivity towards time and space displayed by Gramscian critical theory in international relations and global political economy. Power structures are conceptualized with an emphasis on the interrelationship between political and economic spaces, thus incorporating politically constitutive dimensions of global capitalism and economically constitutive dimensions of global politics. It would be fair to say in this respect that Gramscian critical theory has made major advances towards a political economy of spatiality. Hence it has offered perspectives on globalization and globalizing processes that have, to some degree, conceptualized political economy in direct relation to spatial concerns.[7] Recent Gramscian considerations have included, for example: restructuring of global production processes and resulting changes in work patterns, joblessness and the disintegrative impact on collective labour power and influence; developments in state roles in mediating capitalistic forces, emphasizing private economic possibilities rather than public welfare provision; and intensified global competition involving both states and corporations (Cox 1994, 1995; Gill 1994, 1995, 1997a).

Gramscian analysis has highlighted inequalities within as well as across states (Rupert 1995: 190–1; Gill 1995: 73–4, 77–8), an increasingly prominent feature of the globalized world and one that requires a removal of state-centric blinkers in the approach to spatiality, expanding awareness of the importance of attention to local as well as global forces, circumstances and outcomes. In his recent critique of the heightened 'social Darwinism' of a globalizing 'Anglo-American neoliberalism', Stephen Gill (1995: 77) has noted that 'the already massive gap in income and wealth between the richest 10 per cent and the poorest 10 per cent of the people on the planet increased almost tenfold during the 1980s, according to United Nations statistics'. However, he reminds us that

it is important to remember that the areas and populations who are beneficiaries of the global political economy still represent a small proportion
of the world's population. In this context there is a simultaneous and
interlinked process of incorporation and/or marginalization into/from
the global political economy. This process can be illuminated with reference to the wrenching transitions – involving town and country, agricul-
ture and industry – occurring in much of the Third World.

Spatial relationships and reconfigurations are central to understanding the forces of disintegration and intensification that are characteristic of the contemporary global political economy, as illustrated by the
phenomenon of the global city as a key nexus of power (p. 75), a
subject considered further below. The points raised here demonstrate
the capacities of Gramscian perspectives for revealing why global relations need to be understood in terms of political economy and with a
sensitivity to spatiality that is not constrained by state-centric ontology. Gramscian notions of hegemony contain an attitude towards history which seeks to integrate political and economic power in its
investigation of world orders.[8] The predominant sense of time, and
thus of the relationship of time and space, is related directly to global
capitalism and large-scale developments and trends within it. Major
inequalities are interpreted and mapped in these, rather than state-
centric, terms, and the plight of those with the least power is directly
related to the practical outcomes of dominant ideologies. Issues such
as hunger, mass poverty and environmental degradation feature in
Gramscian understandings of global relations. This is in stark contrast
to the ludicrous ways in which such issues can be overlooked by dominant state-centrism, or treated as separate normative concerns for the
reasons explored in the previous chapter.

Reclaiming/reinventing agency

Agency is vital to critical theory and possibilities for change; thus
Gramscian standpoints, rather than conflating agency and structure
in the manner of neorealism, seek to explore their dynamics. In this
sense, Gramscian approaches to politics are far from abstract, explicitly
in-vestigating the failings of the neoliberal global order, including
loss of legitimacy and problems of social and environmental sustain-
ability, which could open the way for 'counter-hegemonic movement'
(Rupert 1995: 206–7; see also Gill 1995; Gill and Mittelman 1997). Such
perspectives on agency emphasize the potential for collective political
action and the priority of addressing how it might be effective on a global

basis. They also illustrate that the dynamics of contemporary global political economy are characterized by changes in the relationship between political and economic influences, resulting in a lack of clarity about the locations of authority and legitimacy.

The nature of structural change is hard to pin down,[9] and the long-term effects of new social movements focused on a range of issues relating to political economy cannot yet be predicted. It is reasonable to presume that they will have at least some influence on fresh formulations of political and economic engagement and associated processes of legitimization (Camilleri and Falk 1992: 199–235). It is inevitable, in the long term, that new bases for political and economic identities, in the loosest sense, will come to replace those that have been ravaged by recent developments in the global political economy. These continue to affect the relationship between individuals and wider forms of political and economic interest and authority, in ways that have yet to be fully negotiated in theory and practice. What is increasingly clear is that hard-shell notions of states as social containers of citizens are becoming less and less tenable.

Economic security, or should I say insecurity, is one of the major issues here, as the discussion above suggests. The facts of life and death as they have always been suffered by the least powerful in the world are finally gaining some meaning, albeit in a much less drastic fashion, for those who were relying on the continued security of their more prosperous economies (Youngs 1997b, 1997d). This has contributed to increasing strains on, and transformations in, all kinds of social contract, formal and informal, familial, interpersonal and marital, as well as between government and citizen, employer and employed. Such contracts and associated structural conditions are central to established framings of politics and economics, and their destabilization will in turn inevitably disturb these traditional perspectives.[10]

As well as challenging familiar understandings of areas such as authority and legitimacy, and their locations and processes, such developments also involve the testing of political and economic identities associated with them. In these circumstances, questions of agency are fundamental to investigations of change. This is why the critical work that has revealed questions of identity, as discussed in this study, is so crucial to enhancing the conceptualization of global relations. Now I will consider in a little more detail why this is so.

Earlier chapters sought to demonstrate at length the extent to which dominant state-centrism's rational-man-writ-large principles are reductionist and static, ultimately collapsing, through neorealist developments, agency into structure and summing up the whole, ontologically speaking, in terms of deterministic, rationalistic imperatives. These are the parameters of mainstream state-centrism's worldview, the walls of its 'prism' (Ashley 1984: 239). This point cannot be emphasized enough in the interests of clarifying the precise focus of the arguments that have been set out above: on the limitations of dominant state-centrism, on what it cannot see and why.

My investigation has thus sought to highlight the importance of theory/ practice dynamics. In this respect, it follows in spirit much of the critical work considered in adopting a central premise: that the concepts and theories through which we understand the world are not abstracted from it, but are intrinsic to its power structures and processes. Agency/ structure perspectives must be informed by such a critical stance towards knowledge if there is to be awareness of the precise influences of existing forms of knowledge and exactly how they might be challenged where this is felt to be necessary. I have argued that dominant state-centric conceptualizations of international relations require such challenge. The issue of identity is central to this endeavour as a means of breaking state-centrism's static grip on agency/structure conceptualizations, and this task is fundamental to the struggle to make agency an effective category of analysis in international relations and global political economy.

I have sought to make explicit the ways in which dominant patterns of state-centric thought have effaced *open* investigation of agency, effectively keeping it off the agenda as an area requiring attention. Sealed within state-centrism's structural determinism, it has been hidden from analytical view. Richard Ashley (1984: 260) has captured the situation most forcefully in his outstanding critique of neorealist structuralism.

> Far from expanding discourse, this so-called structuralism encloses it by equating structure with external relations among powerful entities as they would have themselves be known. Far from penetrating the surface of appearances, this so-called structuralism's fixed categories freeze the given order, reducing the history and future of social evolution to an expression of those interests which can be mediated by the vectoring of power among competing states-as-actors. Far from presenting a structuralism that envisions political learning on a transnational scale, neorealism presents a structure in which political learning is reduced to the consequence of instrumental coaction among dumb, unreflective, technical-rational unities that are barraged and buffeted by technological and economic changes they are powerless to control.

The critical attempts to rescue us from this kind of abstraction of global relations have represented, in effect, a struggle to reclaim or reinvent the question of agency in international relations and global political economy. This struggle has disrupted abstract notions of politics and political economy, and has grounded them in social relations of power. By asserting, in various ways, politics and political economy as process, it has recognized social dynamics, and thus agency as well as structure. It offers rescue from the temporal and spatial abstractions of dominant state-centrism. It offers rescue from the abstractions of being that are represented by state-centrism's reductive form of individualism. It provides a strong sense of what the world is like without the blinkers that mainstream state-centrism has so effectively provided.

Gender analysis has offered the most radical critiques concerning questions of identity because of its disruption, implicitly and explicitly, of public/private divisions. This move represents a major step forward in the enhancement of conceptualization of global relations. It plays a significant role in making 'global' a meaningful category. It is fundamental to a political economy of spatiality approach which recognizes that political and economic relations do not operate on either side of so-called public/private divides, but _across_ them, and can, in certain respects, be understood to be mutually constituted by them. Gender analysis has demonstrated that social power relations cannot be understood, locally or globally, without addressing the issue of gender, and that the _meanings_ and _effects_ of public/private divisions are vital in this regard. It has already been suggested that such a conceptual position promotes a radical perspective on both political economy and spatiality and their interrelationships: radical, that is, for international relations and global political economy as fields of study. For as V. Spike Peterson and Anne Sisson Runyan's (1993: 9) introduction to their influential assessment of _Global Gender Issues_ explains:

> Gender is not a traditional category of analysis in IR, either in terms of 'what' we study or 'how' we study it. Nor has gender been raised very often as an issue in IR policy-making. In today's world, however, this lack of attention to gender is neither possible nor defensible. As this text illustrates, gender is salient both as a substantive topic and as a dimension of how we study world politics.

And as Simona Sharoni (1995: 150) has argued in her analysis of _Gender and the Israeli-Palestinian Conflict_:

> Gender matters. It shapes both directly and indirectly our relationships, daily practices, and understandings of who we are both as individuals and as part of a broader 'imagined community'. This is a fact that by now should be taken as given. The next time we are asked, in disbelief, to

explain once again what exactly has gender to do with particular developments in world politics, we should turn the question around. Let those who continue to think that gender has nothing to do with politics prove their argument. The burden of proof should not be on those who have learned that gender matters, but rather on those who have made gender invisible and who continue to benefit from this invisibility. We should not waste our valuable time, energies, and resources to demonstrate why gender matters but rather move on to examine exactly how it matters in different contexts.

Attention to gender not only fundamentally alters the approach to power; it does so in direct relation to spatial considerations, and thus has implications for understanding time/space relationships. Gender analysis provides a quite distinct awareness of, and sensitivity to, questions of spatiality, and opens up new possibilities for thinking about time/space linkages. It is distinctive in demonstrating just how radical must be considerations of what is *local*.

Radicalizing spatial understanding of the local: gendered imperatives

Taking *the local* seriously impels recognition of the established partial nature of its interpretation on the basis of the public/private divide, which has featured in social analysis in the past (Okin 1991). For centuries, women have been urging the pertinence and social effects and costs of this divide in clear and forthright terms (Wollstonecraft 1985 (1792)). The private or domestic realm has continued to be a stranger to mainstream analysis of *politics* and *economics*; the causal relevance of the public/private divide to understanding social power relations has been largely overlooked. Despite the renewed interest in the local, it is too readily assumed in terms of the dominant public social parameters, abstracted from concern with public/private social dynamics.[11] But as we all know, the local does not stop at the doorways to our homes; nor, increasingly, does the global. Identities and subjectivities are not, and never have been, constituted in relation to public roles and activities alone. Private, or personal and familial, forms of experience have been essential parts of the process.

Patriarchal power can be understood only with due regard to public/ private separations, their division of gender roles, and the processes of socialization and normalization that maintain them. These processes involve the gendering of social spaces (in public/private terms) and the attachment of identities to them, including through the perception of, as well as actual, differentiated access to, or association with, those spaces.

V. Spike Peterson's (1995) assessment of 'the politics of identity' in relation to democracy, globalization and gender has emphasized how such gendered social hierarchies impact on dominant interpretations of agency: 'conventional accounts of political identity and agency take elite male experience as the norm' (pp. 1–2). This issue is spatial as much as it is institutional and discursive, and it presses home that spatiality and its social articulations and delimitations are central to the interpretation of power *and* the possibilities for change.

If, as I have argued, thinking about local/global relationships must negotiate the public/private issue, then it must take domestic space seriously in ways that mainstream analysis has never done before, and it must do so in ways that take feminist reinterpretations of agency seriously, including with regard to the *personal is political* perspective. For this demonstrates another result of the abstract rational-man-as-actor/agent/citizen principles that are writ large in dominant state-centrism (pp. 12–13). It is an abstraction largely absent of corporeal senses of being, albeit that it may be considered to imply male-centred assumptions in this respect. It treats power relations as if physicality and physical dimensions of interrelationships in the fullest social sense do not need to be accounted for.[12] This is the case with regard to considerations of agency *and* structure.

Gender studies have sought long and hard to disrupt such assumptions by asserting that dominant patterns of socialized and institutionalized gendered behaviour centrally involve physical aspects of identity. Sexual relations, child-bearing and rearing, the role of caring, and gendered notions of physicality are among a host of considerations here. Feminist analysis has increased awareness of how the many *private* involvements of women in social reproduction, particularly of the unwaged kind, have been largely ignored in the focus on the male-dominated *public* roles that are viewed as *sustaining* the political economy and maintaining security for all (Peterson and Runyan 1993: 34–5). The 'gendered division of violence' (p. 90) has been a focus of gender critiques in international relations, which have demonstrated how socially reproduced notions of warrior males and protected females mask the integrated and predominantly unequal roles of men and women in the military-industrial complex. The titles of Cynthia Enloe's influential works in this area strikingly signal the fact that we are dealing with identity and spatiality, with the personal as political, and with political economy as implicating rather than veiling public/private connections and their relevance to power relations: *Does Khaki Become You?* (1983); *Bananas, Beaches and Bases: making feminist sense of international politics* (1990); and *The Morning After: sexual politics at the end of the cold war* (1993).

Gendered dimensions of power are deeply embedded in political economy, as witnessed by the high degree of differentiation in the structure of, and rewards – or lack of them – for, contrasting productive functions and their definitions in societies. The pressures of global re-structuring serve to underline the importance of such considerations and the disproportionately increased burden that results for women in the richer as well as poorer parts of the world. Different aspects of the increasingly important *service sectors* (broadly understood) and the con-centrated role of women within them are important reminders of the analytical weakness of disembodied perspectives on political economy: that is, those which fail to take account of the gendered and bodily nature of work of all kinds.

Whether thinking of the large numbers of females doing the low-grade work that keeps the global financial sector running smoothly (Runyan 1996; Sassen 1991) or the various paid and unpaid domestic and sexual servicing roles of women – including in the growing global prostitution industry – which have prompted Jan Jindy Pettman (1996a, 1996b) to ask whether we should start to think in terms of an 'international polit-ical economy of sex', it is inappropriate to think of *work* without consid-ering the differentiated ways in which minds *and* bodies are involved. Kimberly Chang and Lily Ling (1995) argue, in relation to the role of Philippine domestic workers in Hong Kong, that the female service sector should be recognized as a parallel form of 'explicitly racialized and sexualized' globalization, which acts as a 'crucial facilitator' for the traditionally recognized globalized world of intensified production, financial and media relations and structures.[13] They stress, importantly, that sending and receiving states are 'complicit' in this 'intimate' other side of globalization with its neocolonial characteristics. In my own study of these workers, I have tried to draw out the complex nature in which they relate both public and private contexts in Hong Kong and the Philippines (Youngs 1995a, forthcoming).

> This migrant workforce has played a dual integral role in the develop-ment of the Hong Kong and Philippine economies. In Hong Kong, as in Western economies generally, the participation of women in the labour force has been a growing structural element of both the economy's growth and its transformation to a service orientation (Leung 1995; Wong 1995). The importance of the family in Chinese society has given the public/ private tensions in this respect a high priority in terms of maintaining the *feminized* domestic care role (Ng 1995). The migrant workforce has been crucial as a major *external* solution to this *internal* problem, but the associated public and private connections between Hong Kong and the Philippines are equally important. The migrant domestic workers are key

economic agents for their families at home, regularly sending back goods as well as money, facilitated by their relatively high earning power in the context of their home economy, despite their significantly low status in terms of the Hong Kong economy.

It is fascinating, however, to pay close attention to the _hidden_ nature of these workers as an economic force. In the working week they are predominantly confined to the 'private' domestic space, and their restricted living conditions, whether in their employer's home or otherwise, generally reflect the high premium on space (real estate) in Hong Kong. In terms of their home economies, they are _absent_, returning only as holidays and their visas allow and require, often largely cut off from experiencing their own children growing up. Thus their _absence_ can be understood in both public and private contexts as pervasive. (Youngs forthcoming)

Such perspectives demonstrate the degree to which gender should be considered an integrated and fundamental dimension of analysis of global political economy and globalization, especially with regard to power. Equally importantly, they press home the inadequacies of traditional approaches to political economy that fail to follow through analysis of structural forces and relations in _public_ space to their connections with those in _private_ space. Feminist analysis has a long history of asserting that structure _and_ agency can be understood only by examining the linkages between public and private (Weedon 1987). Globalization has reinforced the power of this assertion and its universal relevance. The implications for understanding structure and agency are subtle and yet to be fully investigated. As this discussion indicates, we are at the stage of clarifying why the issue needs to be on the agenda.

Taking the local seriously, as outlined here, helps to develop a sense of the relationship between time and space.[14] Structure/agency dynamics take on more _intimate_ and _immediate_ characteristics in theoretical and other practical terms. While this has been familiar in considerations of identity and subjectivity in the context of gender analysis, it has not been so in mainstream studies of politics and political economy, which have been dominated by grand senses of historical time and abstract categories of the kinds critiqued in this study. My argument here is that, while taking the local seriously means integrating gender concerns into investigations of global relations, a major result is a new challenge to the analytical sense of time, and one that globalizing processes continue to make an imperative, as I shall explore further in the next chapter.

Gender critiques convince us that key areas such as security, identity and sexuality cannot be neatly separated into public and private, individual and institutional categories. Thus it is essential to investigate connections and tensions across these areas and categories over time.

To conduct such investigations it is vital to look *inside* history in the fullest *social* sense. It is not enough to be inside history to the extent that we observe the decisions of governments and their institutions and the outcomes. It is not enough to be inside history to the extent that we recognize the relevance of developments in global capitalism in such a context. No, it is necessary to go deeper than that and include 'the minutiae of ordinary people's lives' (Enloe 1993: 254). Taking the private seriously when its import in power terms has been veiled for so long is a huge challenge, but a wealth of feminist work can show ways forward. A political economy of spatiality features this as a central premise and celebrates the rich possibilities it opens up. The final chapter explores some of these through a discussion of boundaries and power.

6 | Political Economy of Spatiality

This book depicts a situation in which conceptual rescue is necessary: from the abstractions and associated assumptions of dominant state-centrism. It locates the bases for that rescue in contrasting critical work and its combined influences in undermining those abstractions and assumptions, and revealing their relevance to power and to understanding global relations. The main conclusion is that political economy should be recognized as process, and therefore should be related to spatiality. This approach to political economy seeks to place social relations of power in historical rather than abstract contexts and to explore agency as fully as possible, rather than lock it within structural imperatives. The kinds of question being asked should allow for and investigate dynamism in structure/agency interactions rather than assume a conceptual position that effectively rules this out in any complex fashion. Conceptualizing agency fully must include all kinds of processes and agents, and considerations about *how* they maintain and challenge structural conditions of power. The 'how' is crucial. This involves getting inside the dynamics of power in structure/agency contexts as much as possible. Assuming structurally determined perspectives on power, as is the case in dominant state-centrism, prevents this. The critical arguments detailed in earlier chapters not only provide different means of addressing this problem, but also set out reasons why the task should be undertaken.

It has been implicit that this pushes beyond conceptualizations of power as possession linked to capacity to achieve chosen interests in competition with others, towards analysis of why certain forms of power are accepted, what they are and on what bases their acceptance is constituted (Hindess 1996). The former is characteristic of mainstream state-centric thinking; the latter of the kinds of critical approach considered in this study. The former drives us towards visible demonstrations of power, the latter to less obvious practices of power. The former has a particular purchase on history, emphasizing grand events and structures of conflict, the latter a deeper historical and structural awareness. The former has a partial perspective on who has power and why, the latter a more generalized interest in such issues. The former intensifies power as an abstract category through the conceptual architecture of state-centrism, while claiming a realistic preoccupation with its most brutal articulations in militarism, war and competition; the latter seeks detailed understanding of conflict in the global political economy in a broader and deeply historical sense, including gendered dimensions of conflictual patterns of behaviour that press us to recognize it as *socialized* rather than *natural*, as claimed by rational-man-writ-large principles. The former conceptualizes the world in terms of state-centred notions of power, the latter in terms of social relations of power.

Global / local: rethinking social boundaries

This study examines the degree to which contemporary times are characterized by the rethinking of social boundaries and institutionalized forms of power associated with them. In this regard the state probably remains the key category, but as such it is not an *assumed* state; it is rather one recognized as dynamic and differentiated, one that needs to be explored to be understood. It is interactive with other market forces, institutions and actors, and the forms of these interactions and their effects impact directly and indirectly upon its changing nature as a political entity and, importantly, its relations with its citizens. Neither can the market simply be understood in strictly economic terms, but increasingly needs to be interrogated as a political and cultural arena where production and consumption patterns, work- and life-styles are essential elements of agency/structure considerations.

A political economy of spatiality approach provides a framework for beginning to reconceptualize global relations on the basis that existing definitions of political, economic and cultural spaces are inadequate. State-centric conceptual determinism represents an extreme example of a distorted and misleading worldview based on assumed notions of them. It has been argued that it certainly does not encourage important questions about the dynamism of states, their changing qualities as political and economic forces. The veil that state-centrism draws across our understanding of the world, as this study has outlined, relates directly to restricted definitions of politics, political life and the political individual. Critiques of dominant state-centrism that have been assessed emphasize these factors. The state-centric 'prism', in taking them as given, places them outside the realm of necessary, open investigation. Part of the imperative for breaking apart the prism is to bring these back into view, to spur curiosity about them and about overlapping political, economic and cultural contexts relevant to understanding them.

In the re-examination of influential social boundaries of political, economic and cultural relevance to an understanding of global/local connections, the multidisciplinary debate about the state is growing and diversifying. The fragility as well as the durability of states is of concern (Youngs 1997d): their internal changes in terms of market and community structures, and their joint roles at global levels, including through new technocratic forms of institution such as the World Trade Organization (Hoekman and Kostecki 1995). In these kinds of assessment the state cannot be regarded as a static, eternal category, in the mode of state-centrism's conceptual determinism. It is essentially a dynamic entity whose nature as actor and whose forms of agency, rather than being assumed, require open exploration and reconsideration. And it is in the interaction of political, economic and cultural influences that this dynamism can best be examined, as this chapter will illustrate.

The search is on for new senses of what it means to talk about state governance both within states and in international contexts, as well as better to negotiate the social and spatial remappings of boundaries linked to it.[1] This entails looking at state/market dynamics and major influences shaping them within and beyond individual state boundaries, and exploring the linkages between these phenomena. It involves a sensitivity to the degree to which states are by a wide variety of means working directly and indirectly towards their own transformation. This is happening, for example, through _privatization_ – the increasing transfer of ownership and control of strategic areas, such as health, public transport and telecommunications, from public (collective/state) to private (corporate) hands. Privatization trends have been central to the restructuring of comparatively rich economies like the UK, but they have also been promoted internationally by organizations such as the World Bank as part of structural adjustment routes for developing countries (_Journal of International Affairs_ 1997). Privatization has been among the most dramatic illustrations in recent times of states' self-transformative tendencies, not just in political but also in political-economic, market-related terms. Other similar illustrations have included deregulation – the breaking down of national boundaries with regard to capital movement and financial exchanges. Such developments have characterized the trend for 'market-driven integration' (Drache 1996) in a world where foreign direct investment patterns have remained heavily concentrated in the triad – the USA, Europe and Japan – and transnational mergers have grown in importance, reflecting a continuing concentration of market influence in global corporate networks (UNCTAD 1996; see also Hirst and Thompson 1996).

State/market interactions are bringing about transformations that are integrating political, economic and, to some degree, cultural spaces. Integration is used in a very loose sense here, and there is certainly not a unified global development that can be easily captured by the use of the term. In the broadest sense, it is most applicable to the triad where national and corporate wealth are concentrated and where it is supported by regional forms of integration such as, most notably, the European Union, but also the recently expanded North American Free Trade Association.[2] These stress that there are multilevel forms of state agency that need to be considered because, particularly in the post-1945 period, states have increasingly operated not just as individual actors, but as collective participants in an increasingly complex, influential and overlapping web[3] of regional and global bodies. This web is dominated by the joint influence of the richest countries, led by the USA (Youngs 1999c), and shapes considerations of what may come to be understood as new structures of global governance.[4] The arguments set out here indicate that such considerations demand that we look inside and outside states.

> The strategic spaces where many global processes take place are often national; the mechanisms through which the new legal forms necessary for globalization are implemented are often part of state institutions; the infrastructure that makes possible the hypermobility of financial capital at the global scale is situated in various national territories. The condition of the nation-state, in my view, cannot be reduced to one of declining significance. . . . The state itself has been a key agent in the implementation of global processes, and it has emerged quite altered by this participation. The form and content of participation varies between highly developed and developing countries and within each of these groupings. (Sassen 1996: 27–8)

Far from assuming the state as a bounded social, territorial entity with eternalized forms of sovereignty, as the state-centric prism would perpetuate, it is vital to explore openly *transformations* in its *bounded characteristics*, its *territoriality* and its *sovereignty*. What is most taken as given in state-centrism's conceptual determinism is what is most at issue. Saskia Sassen (1996: 28) argues that sovereignty has been 'decentred' and territory 'partly denationalized', testing 'the explicit or implicit tendency' in the social sciences 'to use the nation-state as the container of social, political, and economic processes'.

> The denationalization of territory occurs through both corporate practices and the as yet fragmentary ascendant new legal regime. . . . Sovereignty remains a feature of the system, but it is now located in a multiplicity of institutional arenas: the new emergent transnational private legal regimes, new supranational organizations (such as the WTO [World Trade Organization] and the institutions of the European Union), and the various international human rights codes. (pp. 28–9)

Sovereignty may still be considered to retain aspects of its mystical eternal qualities as considered in this study, but it cannot be fully understood in practice without a sensitivity to its dynamic and transformative qualities. Sassen's notion of 'an unbundling of sovereignty'[5] indicates that states should be understood in processual terms (p. 29).

The Foucaultian concept of 'governmentality' is helpful in exploring states in this manner because it links government of the self with government of the many, and implicates subjects and thus subjectivity in the processes of government (Foucault 1991a; Gordon 1991; Dillon 1995; Hindess 1996). It identifies modern government, as developed in the West, as being principally about those subjects and its various detailed forms of knowledge about them. As the preface to a recent collection of essays entitled _The Foucault Effect_ (Burchell, Gordon and Miller 1991: x) puts it:

> government is not just a power needing to be tamed or an authority needing to be legitimized. It is an activity and an art which concerns all and which touches each. And it is an art which presupposes thought. The sense and object of governmental acts do not fall from the sky or emerge ready formed from social practice. They are things which have had to be – and which have been – invented.

Foucault's concern with governmentality is one aspect of his broader attempts to de-naturalize the notion of the individual, certainly the notion of the sovereign individual, although one needs to note here that he has been criticized for his lack of attention to gender.[6] His conception of the subject is an active one in the sense of agency; subjects are produced as 'agents' in and through 'an order of knowledgeable practices, norms of conduct, and elaborate protocols of behaviour', and the situation is paradoxical in that it 'involves them as mediums of power in the very exercise of power upon themselves' (Dillon 1995: 324).

Earlier points suggest that, as the bases and forms of governmentality are on the move, so then are the bases and forms of subjectivity, including as expressed through citizenship and political and economic identity.[7] A recent assessment by Nikolas Rose (1996) traces a complex transformation in the 'social' as the collective political sense of identity

in western industrialized states through the increasingly economic definitions of individual autonomy resulting from the transition of respon-
sibilities from state to individual: for example, in health and general
welfare. Rose identifies a disintegration of 'collective' notions of an 'ethical character' into those of multiple 'communities', groups or individuals with diverse interests. This development in governmentality breaks
down collective responsibility into individual responsibility and thus
collective risk into individualized risk.[8] It also breaks down the national
economy into 'zones-regions, towns, sectors, communities' along local/
global relational principles and linked to new rationales associated with
globalization. Rose's assessments emphasize how the very character of
what are understood as the political and the economic is being transformed in direct relation to states and global processes. Such circumstances must be a focus for understanding boundaries, inequality and
power, in relation to theory and practice, in the contemporary world, as
well as for, as Rose indicates, critical thinking about possibilities for
empowerment and challenge.

Inequality and spatiality

The indications are that more thought should be given to the ways in
which states can be considered disaggregated social entities (Youngs
1997b), and that they certainly should not be assumed as *necessarily*
aggregated. It is worth taking account of how the post-1989 situation
has in fact made such attempts at complexity all the more problematic
in conceptual terms. With the falling away of the old bipolar model of
interpreting power in international relations, the linear 'development'
model took prominence. Notions of great power politics and bipolarity
as dominating international affairs held fast for forty years, but as the
1980s passed, a new era appeared to dawn in which the play of global
capital would have a new worldwide field.

Francis Fukuyama's (1992) prediction of the 'end of history' demonstrated that new doors had been opened by the prospects of post-cold
war times, as they quickly became known. His vision of the combined
strength of 'liberal democracy' and 'economic liberalism' as the dominant transnational force of the future was characteristic of the West-
centric 'triumphalism' (Chomsky 1992) that burgeoned in the wake of
the crumbling of the Eastern bloc. In important respects, theses such as
Fukuyama's filled a void in approaches to world affairs, a void largely
conceptual and theoretical.[9] This was related to the limited application
that previous tools of analysis seemed suddenly to have.

Dominant state-centric approaches to international relations had asserted the primacy of politics in defining the nature of those relations (Morgenthau and Thompson 1985; Waltz 1979). This claimed primacy had an overt purchase in cold war times, when the world might be understood in terms of two opposing blocs with two distinct ideological versions of politics (Fukuyama 1992: 251). In the post-cold war situation, according to Fukuyama, there was little standing in the way of the international ideology of liberal capitalism as an increasingly incorporative global destiny. The Fukuyama thesis represents a reframing and restatement of the linear 'development' model of international relations: 'For Fukuyama, economic development, and the scientific and technological factors, the desire for economic growth and the continuing conquest of nature which are associated with it, represent unifying forces in world history' (Youngs 1996a: 65). I have argued that Fukuyama's thesis could be viewed as the ultimate post-cold war discourse of globalization: 'It identifies the progressive imperatives and "homogenising power" of the liberal capitalist system as an irresistible incorporating influence _both_ economically and politically. . . . The "end of history" is presented as a state-centred celebration of the globalization of the Western capitalist system's capacities to meet economic and political needs' (p. 65).

Despite its individual characteristics, the Fukuyama thesis represents a conceptual determinism similar to the dominant forms of state-centrism assessed in this study because it _fixes_ temporal and spatial considerations. Understanding of states and their progress is significantly reduced to their place in the modernization/industrialization league. The main global division is identified as the 'post-historical' part of the world and 'a part that is still stuck in history', broadly speaking between the 'developed' and 'underdeveloped' worlds (Fukuyama 1992: 276, 385). Issues of power and inequality are likewise significantly reduced. Fukuyama's idealized perspective on liberal capitalism fails to reflect the social and spatial complexities of trends of inequality.

There is strong evidence that, while the geographical scope of modernization/industrialization is expanding, the major trend is for greater wealth to be concentrated in fewer hands. As the points made in the first section of this chapter indicate, patterns of inequality need to be studied within as well as across states. The conclusions of the United Nations Development Programme's _Human Development Report_ (1996: iii) explain that over the last fifteen years 'the world has become more economically polarized – both between countries and within countries'. Between 1960 and 1991 the share of the richest 20 per cent of the world's people rose from 70 per cent of global income to 85 per cent, while that of the poorest 20 per cent declined from 2.3 per cent to 1.4 per cent (p. 13). In the past three decades, the proportion of people with per capita income growth of at least 5 per cent a year more than doubled from 12 per cent to 27 per cent, while the proportion experiencing negative growth more than tripled, from 5 per cent to 18 per cent. In sub-Saharan Africa, twenty countries were still below their per capita incomes of twenty years ago (p. 2). In the relatively rich OECD countries, more than 100 million people were below the official poverty line, with the numbers growing in the UK and the USA, among others. Nearly 30 million people were unemployed and more than 5 million homeless (p. 12).

Even in the case of the USA, warnings were sounded relating to increasing income gaps, poverty, job insecurity and the lagging of health care behind economic growth. Between 1975 and 1990, the wealthiest 1 per cent of the population increased its share of total assets from 20 per cent to 36 per cent, and the number of people living below the poverty line is rising, with the per capita income of the poorest 20 per cent less than one-quarter of the country's average income. The UNDP made it clear, too, that even in this relatively successful economy, where jobs were being created, actual job insecurity was increasing because many of these openings were 'dead-end, temporary jobs – without security and without a future'. Employment issues were identified as a major area of concern in respect of eastern Europe and the Commonwealth of Independent States countries, whose populations featured among the 1.5 billion people in about 100 countries with incomes in the 1990s lower than in previous decades, compared with more than 3 billion people in about 60 countries, concentrated in Asia and among members of the Organization for Economic Co-operation and Development, whose incomes were higher than ever before.

Marianne Marchand (1994) has described well some of the complexities of current global inequalities, and the problematics of referring to *North* and *South* as cohesive categories. There is a need to recognize the hierarchical opposition implied by the North–South framing of global relations, the positing of the South as a lesser other to the North, as indicated by the terms '*un(der)*developed countries' and '*less* developed regions'.

> in the very process of discussing and analysing the North–South conflict
> – in particular the nature of the South – African, Asian, and Latin American countries are marginalized. To take this line of thought one step further, this discursive marginalization also leads to political-economic marginalization. And, once set in motion, discursive and political-economic marginalizations reinforce each other. (p. 296; see also Johnston 1991)

Marchand's (1994: 295–7) analysis also indicates that by the 1990s homogeneous views of so-called North and South did not reflect the significance of differences *within* them rather than *between* them, to the point that there had developed 'the distinct possibility of parts of the South finding common cause with parts of the North'. Noteworthy in this respect, for example, are: globalizing pressures associated with the transition from the East–West bipolar framework of political economy; and continuing economic dynamism in East Asia (Vatikiotis 1996; Harris 1990) and its contribution to the increased focus on Asia-Pacific, contrasted with the extremes of poverty in areas such as South Asia and sub-Saharan Africa (UNDP 1997; see also Alexander 1996 and *Alternatives* 1994).

What the subtleties of a perspective like Marchand's make clear is that revised general frameworks for thinking about inequality globally are overdue. This is a major element of the conceptual challenge involved in addressing global relations, and it illustrates the dangers implicit in generalized and hierarchical depictions of the world. The heightened role of the *development* framework as a means of understanding the world in so-called post-cold war times brings with it the need to be aware of the triumph-of-the-West assumption that can so easily be contained within such an approach. In this respect, Fukuyama's 'end of history' thesis is far too uncritical in its celebration of a universal West-centric vision of the future of global political economy. While it celebrates 'the triumph of the technological imperative' as a form of 'global culture' (Youngs 1997a), it fails to probe in any depth, for example, how technologies are contributing to political and economic restructuring of global/local linkages, social and spatial. Communications technologies of all kinds are fundamental to processes of globalization (Mohammadi 1997) – to the expansion and reorganization of investment and production, the growth of trade and new markets for consumption, and the development of the 'service' era where constantly multiplying forms of non-material products, including financial and insurance goods, are exchanged on business-to-business and individual consumer bases.

The phenomenon of the global city – for example, New York, London and Tokyo (Sassen 1991) – has become the motif of new spatial sensitivities that recognize the extent to which the 'compression' of time and space (Harvey 1990) is contributing to the intensification or concentration of economic and to some extent political and cultural influence, socially and spatially. Global cities are regarded as key hubs of transnational financial, corporate, political and cultural power, with, crucially, their linkages playing definitive transnational roles. John Agnew and Stuart Corbridge (1995: 206) have conceptualized 'transnational liberalism' as the new form of hegemony based on differentiated participation in the capitalist world economy. 'Circuits of capital' operate most intensively between major core regions and institutions (including the International Monetary Fund) and secondary regions, with the 'deadlands' of the wealthier economies, the former socialist bloc countries and poorer regions, including sub-Saharan Africa, linked to them mainly by 'provisional circuits of capital'. The Agnew and Corbridge model argues that the new hegemony is 'both polycentric and expansionist' (p. 205).

Such interpretations help to move us beyond the notion of states as bounded political and economic containers, and, importantly, beyond reductively state-centred understandings of power. But it requires approaches that emphasize consumption as much as production and technologized and symbolic aspects of capitalism to take thinking about inequality within as well as between states even further. These demonstrate that temporal, spatial and cultural factors are interacting within processes associated with global capitalism, and that these can be considered globalizing forces in both their market mobility and their universalizing representations, which indirectly and directly peddle mass-product-oriented lifestyles. However, the greatest conceptual challenges are, as studies of cultural imperialism have exposed (Tomlinson 1991), in negotiating the interactions of these space/time/culture associations in specific locations. These are dynamics within dynamics – the meeting of influences with differing degrees of spatial fixity or relevance, and often starkly contrasting temporal and cultural contents.

These cannot be easily investigated without consideration of the living subjects, the consumers or potential consumers, who are the nexus for these diverse influences and who carry them forward in new and integrated forms, contributing to the ways in which the combined influences become institutionalized within societies. Such perspectives, which take economic subjects as seriously as political subjects, and thus recognize the need to consider issues of identity and subjectivity in economic as well as political respects, are centrally concerned with agency/structure dynamics, and their role in understanding global relations will grow.

Richard J. Barnet and John Cavanagh's (1994) book *Global Dreams: imperial corporations and the new world order* captures this imperative through its concentration on the new global age of transnational capitalism, in which entertainment is one of the biggest businesses and growing joblessness is a fact of the future, along with political values fighting an increasingly difficult battle to achieve control over globalizing market and financial forces.

> The emerging global order is spearheaded by a few hundred corporate giants, many of them bigger than most sovereign nations . . . The multinational corporation of twenty years ago carried on separate operations in many different countries and tailored its operations to local conditions. In the 1990s large business enterprises, even some smaller ones, have the technological means and strategic vision to burst old limits – of time, space, national boundaries, language, custom, and ideology. By acquiring earthspanning technologies, by developing products that can be produced anywhere and sold everywhere, by spreading credit around the world, and by connecting global channels of communication that can penetrate any village or neighborhood, these institutions we normally think of as economic rather than political, private rather than public, are becoming the world empires of the twenty-first century. (p. 14)

The distinction between private and public here contrasts with that of gender critiques discussed above, and aligns with the separation in mainstream economic and political analysis of private and public interests. It contributes to the identification of separate economic and political spheres, in which private interests are perceived as dominating the former, and public interests the latter. As the early part of this chapter established, this boundary is increasingly being assessed as one of the central pressure points in considerations of globalization. Barnet and Cavanagh paint a picture of global economic integration coupled with global political disintegration and argue that 'the new world economy' is based on 'four intersecting webs of global commercial activity': 'the Global Cultural Bazaar; the Global Shopping Mall; the Global Workplace; and the Global Financial Network' (p. 15).

Their study is notable for its detailed attention to the interrelated global forces of communications, entertainment, advertising and merchandising. They stress the degree to which the new globalizing economy is a dream machine peddling ideas and concepts that are linked largely to cultural motifs and lifestyles, predominantly those associated with the westernized consumer model. They point out that the 'Global Cultural Bazaar' is the newest of the webs and 'the most nearly universal in its reach' (p. 15), but the 'Global Shopping Mall' is only for the comparatively few.

> Dreams of affluent living are communicated to the farthest reaches of the globe, but only a minority of the people in the world can afford to shop at the Mall. Of the 5.4 billion people on earth, almost 3.6 billion have neither cash nor credit to buy much of anything. A majority of people on the planet are at most windowshoppers. (p. 16)

Indeed, their conclusions contrast the mass involvement in the 'Global Cultural Bazaar' with a much lesser involvement in the other three webs:

'In the new world economy, there is a huge gulf between the beneficiaries and the excluded and, as world population grows, it is widening' (p. 18). The result is a 'crisis' in culture as well as politics, with global economic forces driving spatial definitions of what and who counts in the global marketplace, leaving billions out of the picture and nurturing associative affinities related to these new inside/outside boundaries which have to do more with global cities than states (pp. 19–22).

This kind of analysis develops an expanded awareness of the need to think about inequality in relationship to space, time and culture. Global systems of production and distribution and global financial systems do demonstrate the importance of differences in power to command, utilize and benefit from global space, but the new map of haves and have-nots that results also illustrates the significance of differentiations in territorially associated attachments, levels of mobility and the extent to which that mobility is available purely as a matter of choice. These factors apply whether one talks in terms of companies or individuals, and they are related in major ways to the speed facilitated by communications and information systems.[10] In the contemporary global political economy, with the new commercial and private freedoms these systems have permitted, the definition of space is certainly not solely the preserve of states, and possibly not primarily their preserve, and spatiality must be considered with due regard to economics as well as politics.

Scott Lash and John Urry (1994: 4–5) have pressed thinking in terms of *Economies of Signs and Space*, arguing that we need increased attention to the production of *'signs'* rather than 'material objects', and to 'economic life', addressing 'reflexivity' in relation to both production and consumption. Their analysis identifies the haves and have-nots in direct relation to the *'information and communication structures'* that represent the economies of signs and space. For those who have them and who are concentrated most obviously in the richer parts of global cities such as London and New York, the result is increasing 'aesthetic reflexivity', which can be the basis for 'critique' as well as cultural (and social) reproduction (pp. 6–8 and 142–3). It is not possible here to indicate their detailed arguments, merely to set out some broad indicators from my understanding of them. They delineate inequality socially and spatially, and to some extent on the basis of time/space freedoms or restrictions, with concentrations of extremes of the information-and-communications rich and poor within cities, classified variously and including those that have been deindustrialized and restructured.[11] These extremes in what they term 'post-organized capitalist economies' are reflected in widely differentiated levels of reflexive possibilities shaped in relation to both work and wider activities: 'Post-organized capitalist society is the two-thirds society, in which the gap between the increasingly reflexive service class and the skilled working class is increasingly separated from that of the so-called "under-class"' (p. 57).

Inequalities in this framework of analysis are directly linked to varying capacities to associate time and space, including through cultural experience and consumption. Lash and Urry argue that there are changes in the nature of structure and agency forcing structural imperatives into agency through an 'accelerating individualization process' (p. 5), which brings most benefits and possibilities for empowerment to those with greatest reflexive scope. This scope is partly defined by an intensity of time duality as 'instantaneous' as well as 'evolutionary', both of which are captured by 'science and technology as social structural practices', instantaneous experience of time having been facilitated by developments such as computer and communications systems as a result of centuries of scientific and technological developments (pp. 223–51). 'Aesthetic reflexivity' is fuelled by the cultural mobility that such systems, and products and services associated with them, permit through journeys of the mind as well as the body, resulting in a 'cosmopolitanism' that cannot be understood along state-centred lines (pp. 256, 281).

While Lash and Urry's focus is mainly the so-called advanced industrialized countries, their extensive assessment of the new 'under-class' in the USA and Europe presses home the importance of considering inequality with spatial sensitivities that are non-state-centric and truly transnational. Lash and Urry describe this class restructuring as a kind of process of disempowerment or, as they term it, 'a sort of structural downward mobility' (p. 145) for those pushed towards the bottom. The 'under-class', including international migrants working in 'a new downgraded manufacturing sector in the advanced economies', are concentrated in the 'impacted ghettoes' of cities (pp. 145–60). Lash and Urry's view of the 'global order' of the future is one 'consisting of multiple and overlapping networks of power', with states being 'squeezed between global and local processes' and losing their status as 'obvious and legitimate sources of authority over civil society'. They identify the possibility for new forms of 'cosmopolitan democracy' (pp. 281, 301; see also Held 1993, 1995).

This study's earlier discussions indicate that, while the themes Lash and Urry set out and the detail with which they investigate them are illuminating, they do not go far enough in their framing of 'globalization and localization'. They fail to reveal the integrated importance, to understanding space/time relations, of patriarchal structures globally and locally, and, as already argued, the extent to which the local has already been determined along patriarchal lines with public/private hierarchies embedded within it.

Space / time relations and patriarchal structures

Gendered aspects of social relations of power are fundamental to understanding what the global and the local are. For example, cultural consumption cannot be considered in isolation from the multiple gendered factors that drive it, including through the social construction of households and identities. Public and private forms of consumption – who consumes what, how and why – are gender issues. What is more, both notions of 'instantaneous' and 'evolutionary' time are essential to assessments of inequality in this regard, for two reasons. The first is that the so-called development model framing perspectives on global history has had the effect of naturalizing a particularistic version of 'evolutionary' time on a universalistic basis. This results in the spatial and hierarchical categorization of the globe in relation to stages along a vertically conceived development scale. I would argue that prioritization of this critical problem remains central to future thinking about, and the development of, strategies of political economy to address the pressing tensions between continuing and embedded global capitalist expansionary processes and their human and environmental costs. Gender issues come into play in complex ways, because patriarchal structures, including those affecting all kinds of institutional processes defining the differentiated power between men and women, continue to impact on how science and technology have developed, who has been able to influence their applications and priorities, and how the resulting goods and services are marketed (Harding 1991).

Secondly, as Lash and Urry helpfully explain, 'evolutionary' time and 'instantaneous' time are intimately connected; thus it is important to consider notions of 'instantaneous' time in relation to the household colonization of private – that is, *domestic* – female time. This is a fascinating area that globalization studies have opened up in regard to gender inequalities. A few brief points only can be made here. In their assessments of public/private divides, feminists have long emphasized the lack of personal space that dominates women's lives in the home, and, as women's social roles and subjectivities have been mainly defined and influenced by their association with the private or domestic sphere, and they have been given limited access to the public domain, the outcome is clear. Women have been, with variations in different social and geographical contexts, and in contrasting as well as complementary ways, oppressed through a limitation on their experience of instantaneous time. In the past, this form of time might have involved the pursuit of any kind of personal interest or activity with individual or social relevance.

Nowadays this would also be the case, but the increasing focus of much of consumption on high-technology products and services, particularly those involving computers, requires the addressing of gendered distinctions between knowledge of, use of, ability to own, and time to experience such facilities.

The expanding age of the double burden for women, when they must work both in and outside the home, and when most, if they are using computers at all, will be doing so for low-grade inputting tasks (Runyan 1996), highlights the growing importance of this situation. Consumption as well as production are fundamentally gendered and it is vital to take this into account when thinking of processes of globalization. I would argue that this requires the development of an acute awareness of the importance of different forms of patriarchal time. The dynamics of globalization should be regarded as, among other things, a dynamics of patriarchal forces, in which influences that have different historical and geographical roots converge. It is the interaction of these forces, in particular places at particular times, that reveals some of the deepest aspects of the dynamics of inequality at work in globalization. The kind of analysis that Lash and Urry have undertaken is, with all its subtleties towards time and space, essential for developing thinking about globalization, but I would assert that it is important to go further and get _inside_ globalization as discussed here.

I have concentrated on talking about women and I make no apologies for that. However, patriarchy is about inequalities not only between men and women, but also between men and men; furthermore, it is about inequalities between women and women, and men and men, across different social and geographical contexts. In all respects, these inequalities should be addressed in their various formal and informal guises.[12] By way of processes associated with production and consumption, transnational capitalism is an expression of many of these forms, including through policies and practices of corporations, and institutions such as the World Bank and the International Monetary Fund. When global meets local, or vice versa, patriarchal forces also meet, and the complexity of the ways in which they may negotiate and reinforce one another or be in tension with one another is conceptually daunting. One thing that certainly should be understood is that there are multiple mobilizations of political, economic and cultural factors that have different historical and spatial associations.

As a recent collection of essays (Pearson and Leung 1995b) indicates, the past and present of Hong Kong demonstrates such situations. In Hong Kong, gendered forms of capitalistic production and consumption meet British colonial and Chinese patriarchal forces, and developments preceding the transfer of the territory to China in July 1997, such as democratic reform, provided new assertions of the unequal position of women (Pearson and Leung 1995a). The double load for women inside and outside the home is clear here.

> the family is accepting of a wife and mother working as long as she con-
> tinues to maintain her domestic responsibilities. Neither the institutions
> of work nor the family wish to make changes to accommodate these dual
> demands. Thus, even working-class men, however much they are exploited
> at work, can look forward to coming home as a cessation of work. For a
> woman, coming home is exchanging one kind of work for another: cook-
> ing, cleaning, washing, and supervision of homework. (p. 8; see also Ng
> 1995)

The position of women in Hong Kong illustrates how centuries-old traditions and institutionalized structures meet more recent and chang-ing forms of capitalism in global/local interactions. These circumstances affect the nature of women as agents of change in Hong Kong, in ways that both assert the success and mutual reinforcement of combined patriarchal forces and present challenges to them (Leung 1995; Tsang 1995). In respect of the latter, consciousness raising has been of major importance.

> For many community and social workers, services catering to women have
> fast become a necessity, as real problems generated by women's contra-
> dictory social roles become pressure points in the local community. More
> women are recognizing these contradictory demands too, by complain-
> ing out loud to social surveyors, by joining the proliferating women's
> groups at the local level, and by participating in campaigns that once
> appeared too 'political' for them. (Tsang 1995: 286)

One of the key areas in such global/local contexts is the combination of patriarchal forces relating to the social construction of female identity, and there is no doubt that this is image-intensive, whether one thinks of mass cultural media such as film, various forms of pornography (Dworkin 1981), or advertising (Hennessy 1993). Different spatial, his-torical and cultural locations are involved in considering all these areas. It is fair to say that mainstream social analysis has only relatively recently paid attention in any major way to issues of representation and power, which have been a long-established dimension of feminist critique. Representations are constructed and institutionalized through a variety of means: discursive and other social practices, as well as the actual presentation and contextualization of images themselves (Weedon

1987). Feminists have long asserted the need to consider multiple re-inforcement in this respect across social institutions and processes, legal, political, economic, religious and cultural. This need is further reinforced and made more complex analytically in an age of increasing global/local interactions and 'the circulation of images on a novel global scale' (Lash and Urry 1994: 301).

The pervasive nature of gender construction through such imagery deserves primary attention,[13] particularly in the light of the growing global sex industry and multiple and culturally diverse reinforcement and commodification of women as objectified service-providers and consumers, as objects of sex and violence (Pettman 1996a, 1996b; Pearson and Yu 1995). I would not want to suggest in this discussion, however, that I am thinking solely in terms of women as static – that is, geographically fixed – in relation to global/local processes. Women must also be considered mobile, even if, as is most often the case, they are in disadvantaged positions, as Chang and Ling's (1995) assessment discussed in the previous chapter makes clear.

A recent collection of essays edited by Audrey Kobayashi (1994b) on *Women, Work, and Place* reveals that such considerations should not be confined to very recent history. This collection also explores usefully detailed reasons for ensuring that issues of inequality are addressed in 'multicultural' ways, thus relating political, economic, class and gender considerations to those of race or ethnicity (Kobayashi et al. 1994: xiii). Kobayashi's (1994a) own assessment of the early-twentieth-century position of Japanese 'picture brides' in relation to their country of origin and their new country of residence, Canada, maps a global/local network of multiple forces of gendered, sociocultural and racial oppression, and deeply culturally oriented forms of agency in addressing such experience. 'Picture marriages' were arranged in connection with constraints on continuing Japanese male immigration, official attempts to stabilize the existing community of Japanese immigrants, and familial obligations on the male and female sides (pp. 54–5). Kobayashi's account of this situation, based on interviews with women involved as well as readings of their traditional poetic forms of expression, recounts mixed feelings of loss, fear, obligation, loyalty and achievement.

> For women disembarking in Vancouver, the most painful aspects of adaptation to a new life began. First the shy initial encounter with a husband. Some found that the husbands matched their expectations, while others found that the husbands had sent photographs of younger or more handsome friends. Within twenty-four hours came the humiliating experience of being whisked to a drygoods shop to shed the Japanese-style kimono

that was a mark of shame to those already living in Canada and to replace it with a Western-style dress over (for the first time) underwear and a corset; thence to the beauty salon to dismantle the Gibson-girl hairstyle current in Japan at the time but deemed ridiculous and overdone in turn-of-the-century Vancouver and ultraconservative Victoria. (p. 57)

Kobayashi tells of the hardships encountered by these women in relation to: their personal lives; their work and its traditionally under-valued social place in comparison with the role of mother; and 'instit-utional and systemic racism' (pp. 62–3).

It is impossible to do justice here to the intricate conceptual messages that the kind of analysis Kobayashi undertakes in this essay commun-icates with regard to thinking about global/local dynamics and their varied historical and sociocultural linkages and locations. However, this brief reference to them serves as a reminder of the multifaceted nature of inequality, relating to issues of identity and subjectivity, and the in-teraction of different historical and spatial influences.

Postcolonial analysis is perhaps the most notable field to have pressed these points, particularly with regard to cultural reproduction through texts identified as fiction as well as history (see references in note 1 of chapter 5; see also Young 1990; Darby and Paolini 1994). This kind of analysis has facilitated perspectives on societies as historically con-structed, including through diverse social and discursive practices and strategies that interrelate, often in extremely complex and intimate ways, places that may be geographically distant, but which are connected through power relations, the colonial form being probably the most ob-vious example. In such contexts, societies are being investigated in terms that are spatially as well as temporally dynamic. In other words, inter-pretation of them is undertaken in relation to historical *and* geopolitical and geocultural considerations. Multiple inequalities – for example, of race, class or social hierarchy, and gender – can be taken into account (Darby 1997; Pettman 1996b). The need to consider differentiated in-volvement in and experience of processes of globalization is empha-sized, as is the importance of paying greater attention to the specifics of local conditions in contexts of the so-called Third World or South.

I indicated earlier, in my critique of Fukuyama's 'end of history' thesis, the dangers of West-centric universalizing tendencies of discourses of globalization, particularly in such a state-centric and reductive form (Youngs 1996a). Postcolonial analysis has warned that such developments threaten to distance us even further from detailed understanding of the poorer parts of the world and agency/structure issues relevant to them. This point expands further the multifaceted claims of this chapter for deep, critical and dynamic attention to the local, especially in considerations of inequality.

'Subjects in the Third World (or anywhere else for that matter) cannot simply imagine away material barriers of inequality and dependency. On the other hand, such material factors do not deny a space for navigation and innovation on the part of individuals and cultures in marginalized positions of power' (Paolini 1997: 51). Sinith Sittirak (1996) is one such innovator. Her exploration of 'the stories of women and the changing environment in Thailand' involved a powerful rediscovery of the local and the most personal of critical engagements with public/private social hierarchies of multiple local and global origins. Her investigation of 'development' led her both to discover how _her_ knowledge on the subject had been 'colonized' and, with the help of _her mother's_ knowledge, towards a process of 'decolonizing' herself.

> through the process of dialoguing with my mother, I found that being socialized into the mainstream educational system during the 'development era' had alienated me from my own mother. What is worse is that I had misunderstood her; to me, she was just another old-fashioned, rural woman. I felt ashamed of my own roots. To be unmodern (read: unwestern) was not acceptable. I felt so embarrassed, as a child, to use my mother's home-made and hand-made bamboo ruler at school, instead of the plastic rulers others were using. . . . After the imposition of several decades of western development on Thai society, our traditional values and knowledge have become marginalized. How often in my life have I heard my mother recall ecological tips taught to her by her grandfather (my mother had been orphaned as a little girl). The environmental knowledge that she continues to carry with her and tries to pass on to us is several generations old. Instead, it is devalued and ignored, as we have been told to do. My generation has been encouraged to learn everything from 'out there' but nothing about our own traditional knowledge. Who would dare to quote our great-grandparents as a reference in graduate school? To cite from the World Bank Annual Report is much more sophisticated and secure, in terms of 'accepted' knowledge. (Sittirak 1996: 146)

Conclusion

The two chapters in this part of the book have discussed a political economy of spatiality approach as a promising framework for recontextualizing agency/structure considerations in post-state-centric modes of analysis. They identify the importance of expanded and critical considerations of spatiality as central to new forms of understanding of political-economic interactions, and highlight the fundamental role of gender perspectives in this area. These offer the potential for opening up consideration of local/global linkages and contexts with deep sensitivity to historical and contemporary influences that have shaped social relations of power on the bases of gender. The detail of the arguments put forward, particularly in this chapter, has illustrated that this is a vital means to achieve fresh and dynamic perspectives on the specifics of global relations.

Throughout part III there has been strong focus on the state as a category that is at the centre of critical thinking about globalization. However, the approach to the state has been far distant from the conceptual determinism of dominant state-centrism and its assumptions about political economy. The intention, among other things, has been to demonstrate how much more effective our reconsiderations of the state and global relations can be if we abandon the state-centric prism. In this respect, states are viewed in relation to political and economic processes in which they are an integral, but not necessarily always definitive, part; in which they are dynamic rather than static, and thus transformative rather than predetermined. I have stressed the need to look inside states as well as outside them, partly at least in order to examine their self-transformative tendencies. These concern political and economic developments, understanding of which can be gained through attention to processes of political and economic restructuring and the impact on locales and regions, communities and individuals.

Citizenship has been identified as a key category in the negotiation of change in global/local contexts and the pressures on existing forms of political and economic authority and accountability. Earlier chapters have stressed the degree to which the citizen has remained conceptually encapsulated within the state as container in dominant state-centrism. Substantial grounds for smashing apart the prism lie in the need to access citizens as implicated and active participants in processes of globalization, including those associated with consumption as well as production. Emphasis on consumption as well as production draws close attention to the socially and spatially gendered characteristics of public/private divides and constructions. The radical potential of gender critiques for sophisticated and spatially as well as temporally aware negotiations of the local has been illustrated in some detail. I have argued that new thinking about agency and structure relies not only on perspectives that recognize social relations as dynamic, that reject assumptions of the state as a territorially bound social container, and that open up broader spatial investigations of political-economic processes, but also on the *deepening* of analysis of political and economic categories themselves, including state, market and citizen, to reveal that dominant patriarchally driven theoretical and other forms of practice fail to address the public/private questions so vital to understanding power.

I have stressed that dominant perspectives such as state-centrism present a version of reality that abstracts the public world of institutional activity and power from the public/private dynamics that play a fundamental role in both the precise forms, and capacities for perpetuation, of that power. This version reifies the public over the private, the public presence over the private absence. I have argued that, even in the most complex forms of analysis of local/global associations, such as that undertaken by Lash and Urry (1994), this static social perspective can still be found to endure. This is not necessarily surprising and can be taken to reflect at least in part the realities of historically entrenched patriarchal power in theoretical as well as other forms of practice. That the public world can be taken as a given and _full_ account of social reality can surely be recognized as an embedded patriarchally driven form of 'common sense', one which this study has sought to attack directly. The position I have outlined signals public/private dynamics as essential to deep investigations of spatiality and social relations of power, and as a central and integrated part of the challenge of enhanced conceptualizations of global relations. I have emphasized identity and subjectivity issues as part of this picture and suggested how close concern with public/private dynamics will assist investigations into political and economic transformations, including those associated with gendered patterns of production and consumption and associated knowledge processes.

The Conceptual Challenge: Concluding Thoughts

Three conceptual trajectories for the future have been outlined. The first represents the toughest and most diverse challenge: the removal of state-centric blinkers. It is the revelation of states as dynamic social entities subject to transnational forces for change that must be understood internally as well as externally. If the character of states is undergoing significant transformation, and there are strong indications that this is the case, this conceptual direction is not only essential, it is urgent. Secondly, it is necessary to break down the superficial paradigmatic barriers that have inhibited critical thinking in international relations and global political economy, and which have stood too strongly in the way of capacities to address the fundamental conceptual blindness that entrenched state-centric dispositions have imposed. Thirdly, this should be used as a new basis for negotiating the relevant and rich multidisciplinary insights awaiting attention in respect of global relations, and for understanding the processes that are driving and defining them. New combined perceptions, which extensive traditions of analysis of the international/global and critical interactions in international relations and global political economy have provided, can then be brought to this cross-disciplinary scene. In the last two areas, the achievements of gender critiques have been identified as the most profound in addressing power, inequality and globalization in new ways that demonstrate multiple sensitivities to time and space.

Seeing states afresh

I am suggesting a move on from the stale and limited debates about the status of states, based on abstractions which, from the start, prevent the negotiation of them in diverse and meaningful ways in theory and practice. It is important to admit that state-centrism has told us all too little about the complex characters of states, their differences as well as their similarities across the globe, and the commonalities and distinctions in the changing bases for, and forms of, their legitimacy and authority. I am arguing that the partiality of the state-centric perspective be taken for what it is: a view of international relations that is informative only up to a point, and highly misleading if this point is taken as the ultimate conceptual destination. It is important to recognize that neorealist developments have taken state-centrism's conceptual colonization into the area of political economy, with drastic results for the possibilities of open appreciation of the ways in which politics and economics interact on global and local levels. This has led to a situation where state-centric blinkers not only prevent perceptions of politics in any dynamic and expansive sense, but have a similar impact on approaches to political economy.

The neorealist turn has been portrayed as a double disaster in this sense, and its structural determinism is analytically a fatal endpoint that must be avoided at all costs. If this is not achieved, mainstream thought runs the risk of increasing distance from the dynamics that explain not only the transformative aspects of global relations, but also the objects it claims are of central interest – states.

This is not just a matter of theory. Dominant traditions of academic work in international relations and global political economy have always been closely associated with highly influential realms of practice – the worlds of diplomacy, finance, commerce and think tanks. In all these areas, the motivations for improved understandings of international/ global processes are stronger than ever and increasingly varied. As our impressions of the speed at which such processes are moving deepen, the practical imperatives for their accurate assessment are continually reaffirmed. Such concerns dominate bureaucracies at national, local and global levels as much as they do boardrooms and finance houses. The range of issues, goals and concerns is vast. The need for sophisticated forms of knowledge and understanding is growing at a scale that is hard to comprehend. And policy has never been the sole preserve of the powerful. Those working towards greater equality in global and local contexts need more than ever before to be able to interpret the complex linkages between those contexts, how they are being pressured and what may be the outcomes. The imperatives for adequate assessments of global relations are growing, the diversity of the audiences for them greater with every year that goes by.

While the task of predicting the next global location of capitalist growth, and the nature of that growth, is preoccupying companies, large and small, and executives, managers and financiers around the world, there are organizations, and dedicated paid and voluntary workers, coping with and addressing the human and environmental fall-out that is the downside of the global capitalist dream and its expansionary characteristics. Campaigns, whether for capitalist or planetary survival, are mobilized on global and local bases, and require concepts and theories adequate to all their needs. States are central participants in these times of global change, and they are having to cope with the resulting problematics. They never have been static social entities, but now, more than ever, this is being revealed in their explicit negotiation of political and economic policies in direct relation to global factors.

There is no doubt that the political and economic identities of states are under strain. Questions of security are central; the broad contract between citizen and state has traditionally been fashioned on the basis of this concept in theory and practice. The nuclear era marked the first major crack in the security shield, and the developing realities of the increasingly global economy have penetrated it further. Now notions of global rather than national identities are looming large, with new forms of cosmopolitanism based on greater political, economic and cultural mobility for new elites. Contract between citizen and state may still retain its largely traditional form, but no one can doubt that it is being tested. Its current structure may hold firm for some time, but transformations within it may arise unexpectedly and, perhaps, sooner rather than later. Static notions of the state are as good as useless in such circumstances. I argue for facing that and grasping with enthusiasm the conceptual opportunities offered by criticisms of them.

Thinking collectively

The way forward is clear – much of the relevant theoretical work has already been done. It is simply a case of making it possible to take full advantage of it. In the terms of this study, doing so involves abandoning the chains of superficial paradigmatism, which obscure the necessary connections and prevent the pursuit of them openly and collectively. Such connections enable a deep theoretical gaze into states to see the people and diverse social processes that make them a reality. They encourage a recognition that politics is about process and that the detailed power of the state must be understood through its internal as well as its external manifestations. They prompt questions about the relationship between individual and state identity, and the ways in which the two have become mutually dependent as articulated by and through complex practices, including those of the theoretical kind. They facilitate awareness of patriarchal forces operating across political economy: forces structured and institutionalized, some with long histories, and which are globally, nationally and locally located. They indicate that abstractions can be as dangerous as they may be conceptually useful. They can hide perhaps even more than they reveal, certainly when it comes to issues of inequality.

The rational-man-writ-large principles of dominant state-centrism are a perfect demonstration. Their distorted conceptualizations of the individual/the agent are among the characteristics most responsible for state-centrism's analytical weakness and extreme prejudice. Gender critiques have exposed this, but they have fallen foul of superficial paradigmatism. Their fate has been too often the conceptual ghetto. This volume has sought to emphasize that gender analysis is not just another way of looking at global relations, a different perspective. It is a fundamental challenge to established patriarchal patterns of thinking about politics and economics across all social settings. It articulates the multiple and institutionally entrenched biases in such thinking, and it provides whole new bases for it.

I argue that both critical and mainstream theorists in international relations and global political economy need to take note of this point – gender considerations cannot just be added on; they need to be analytically integrated. To spell it out simply, gender refers to men as well as women; it is not a supplementary form of analysis to be regarded as women's work. It is hardly surprising that, in such male-dominated areas as international relations and global political economy, the championing of gender as a serious analytical cause has had to be undertaken by a series of dedicated and determined female theorists. But now that they have laid such excellent groundwork, it should become a collective endeavour to build upon it and take the work forward in as many comprehensive, diverse and powerful ways as possible.

This book has provided a small glimpse of the provocative and vital conceptual directions that gender analysis has revealed. They are genuinely innovative and strike to the heart of concerns about globalization and the need to get inside the processes that characterize it, to understand how they work and who is involved when and where. Gender critiques have been at the forefront of attacks on the fundamental paradigmatism of dominant state-centrism. They have provided some of the clearest and most people-oriented, including, of course, women-aware, statements of its damaging distortions and blindness. They have already made their mark on new thinking about global relations by affirming repeatedly that, if global is to be meaningful, it must represent global human experience, including that of women in all manner of social position, across all countries of the world. These critiques have done most to remake international relations and global political economy as academic fields oriented towards full and expanding, rather than partial and limited, awareness of social relations of power.

Gender analysis and global relations: the power of theory and practice

In global times, academic interests increasingly overlap. Multi disciplinary work on the state, global capitalism and culture is growing. The boundaries between academic areas of study are breaking down, opening up new potential for exchange. The focus of this book on mainstream and critical thinking about the state and sovereignty has borne this in mind. I have anticipated that it will have a multidisciplinary audience and I have written it in the belief that there is much to share, including awareness of mistakes that have already been made and the grounds on which these may be understood. I have provided examples of insights that international relationists and global political economists can draw from other disciplinary endeavours. These have mainly related to the problem of understanding change and the consequent importance of developing conceptualizations of time and space. But another message is that there is a general need to prioritize attention to the achievements of gender critiques in these areas.

Gender analysis has always been geared towards change. It is intrinsically about understanding power, who has it, on what basis, how it works, and its results. It has asserted that politics and economics, that political economy, is about people, that power is not some abstract category, but one that must be understood on the basis of historically constituted social relations that feature commonalities as well as specificities related to different times and places. Feminist analysis has always demonstrated a profound sensitivity to spatiality and power, recognizing, notably through its investigations of public/private divides and their consequences, that social practices are always located spatially as well as temporally, and that this has implications for questions of identity and subjectivity, as well as for associated processes of socialization. Feminists were the first to assert influentially that politics relates to the private as well as the public sphere and that agency is a privately as well as a publicly constructed phenomenon. Feminist politics, with its overt emphasis on the personal, has never kept issues of agency and structure at an abstract distance. It has been a politics of the here and now, one that has negotiated change on immediate and personal fronts, continually and actively, in theory and practice, validating the structural and long-term effectiveness of incremental agency/structure interactions, large and small. Feminist politics has been increasingly global, addressing tensions as well as commonalities across distinct cultural and social settings. Differentiated power among women, locally, nationally and globally, is a central concern addressed once again in theory and practice.

Feminists and supporters of their causes over centuries have contributed to changing perceptions of the very nature of politics. Recently they have worked to transform perceptions of global politics and global political economy, taking the rich insights of long traditions of thought where they are much needed. I have argued that multidisciplinary interests in globalizing processes, particularly those which press us to reconsider the approach to power on the basis of time/space linkages, have much to gain from this critical work. Mainstream social analysis has traditionally concentrated on grand historical, social and geopolitical framings of time and space, but has recently been searching for more diverse, subtle and immediate senses to address the effects of the highly technologized commercial, financial, communications and commodification systems characteristic of contemporary processes of global capitalism.

Among many things, feminist social analysis has offered differentiated sensitivities to time and place. These have now taken on new global significance. I have argued that future thinking about political economy will need to address patriarchal forces as dominant dynamic factors. We now live in an era when in any one place, at any one time, such factors, with varying temporal and spatial, historical and political, economic and cultural associations, are interacting. Understanding these patriarchal dynamics and how they are changing the nature of global inequalities is one of the prime conceptual challenges we face.

Notes

Chapter 1 Embedded State-centrism: From Realism to Neorealism

1 The abandonment of the dollar–gold standard and the move to a floating exchange rate system should not be understood simply in terms of a comparative weakening of US economic power. In referring to the decisive Nixon measures of August 1971, Herman Van der Wee (1987: 479) has argued that they 'did not in any way imply that the United States was ceding its monetary hegemony over the West. On the contrary, the intention was to strengthen this hegemony, though on new foundations.' See the full discussion by Van der Wee (pp. 421–512).

2 With regard to neoliberal institutionalist preoccupations with interdependence (Keohane and Nye 1989 (1977)), Robert Keohane (1993: 285) has argued that it is a continuing promoter in so-called post-cold war times of the growth in 'the number and complexity of international institutions'. A wide-ranging discussion of interdependence in theoretical and substantive respects and in direct relation to globalization has been undertaken by Barry Jones (1995).

3 Michel Foucault's work on the history of theory encourages the search for both continuity and discontinuity, recognizing that the former may not always be immediately evident (see Foucault 1966, 1969; see also Der Derian 1991 and J. George 1994).

4 This is very much a Foucaultian point. See Foucault's (1969) discussion of theoretical 'transformations' and the importance of considering how past theoretical traces may be retained over time in new theoretical forms.

5 For examinations of individualism and structuralism, see, for example, Keat and Urry (1982). See also Sayer (1992).

6 The import of the gender implications of this form of theorizing has been extensively discussed. See, in particular, Peterson (1992a) and Di Stefano (1991).

7 On Hobbes and international theory, see Vincent (1981).

8 See the discussion of associated issues in Ashley and Walker (1990).

9 The following examination of Hobbes's *Leviathan* was first undertaken in Youngs (1990).

10   The question of where exactly we should locate modernity historically is complex. The post-Enlightenment period's emphasis on rationality is certainly important (see Walker 1993: 9–11; see also King 1995). For a discussion of state, society and modernity, see Albrow (1996).

11   Of interest here is Walker's critique of what he terms Waltz's 'extreme structuralism', in which 'Waltz is able to both insist on a sharp distinction between politics within states and relations between them and to deploy a universalising account of instrumental rationality that he believes to be equally applicable to states systems, tribes, oligopolistic firms and street gangs' (p. 134). See also Ashley's (1988b) discussion of 'vertical' and 'lateral' images of international relations.

12   See Alexander Wendt's (1987: 336) footnote on different approaches to 'structuration theory'. Anthony Giddens's (1979, 1984, 1994) work in this area has been particularly influential. See also Craib (1992) on Giddens's arguments.

13   Michel Foucault's analysis of discourse and power is helpful in this respect (see Foucault 1971; see also Der Derian and Shapiro 1989).

Chapter 2   *Conceptual Determinism Revealed*

1   The work of authors such as Theda Skocpol (1979) and Michael Mann (1986, 1993) has examined from contrasting perspectives the historical developments of states in international contexts.

2   Ashley (1984: 276–9) argues for 'a *dialectical competence model*' that 'would preserve classical realism's rich insights into international political practice while at the same time exposing the conditions, limits, and potential for change of the tradition in which classical realism is immersed'. There is not space to go into this in more detail here, but it is important to note the emphasis on the critical reflection on realism as a form of knowledge in a theory/practice context.

3   For a full understanding of Ashley's position, it is necessary to consider the arguments of his earlier work referred to here.

4   Some may view this as too forceful an attack on neorealist variant neoliberal institutionalism, which emphasizes 'the role of international institutions in changing conceptions of self-interest' with regard to states (Keohane 1993: 271). However, as has been argued earlier, this variant adheres to neorealism's state-centric ontology and thus remains fundamentally trapped within its conceptual prism. The distinctions between neorealism and neoliberal institutionalism may be important, but it could be argued that the recent attention given to the 'debate' between them reflects a narrowing rather than a broadening of ontological focus when compared with the earlier critical discussions surrounding neorealism, upon which this study draws. The two key collections here are Keohane (1986a) and Baldwin (1993b). See also on this specific point, Baldwin (1993a).

5   Maclean (1988: 300) stresses that 'empiricist epistemology' crosses the so-called great debate divide between traditional and scientific theorizing.

6 Jan Aart Scholte (1993) has undertaken an interesting and detailed discussion of associated issues.
7 Strange's work is often referred to as 'eclectic' (see Strange 1991).
8 This is a complex area. See Cerny's (1995) extensive discussion of public and private goods. The traditional notion of public goods has been influential in the idea of 'regimes' in the post-1945 global political economy (see Krasner 1983). There are a range of concerns, including those relating to ecology and the environment, which have expanded the debate about international public goods (see Commission on Global Governance 1995).

Chapter 3 _Beyond Superficial Paradigmatism_

1 Reference here is Lapid (1989: 236). See also Hollis and Smith (1991: 16–44), Holsti (1985) and Olson and Groom (1991). In broad terms, post-positivist work challenges the ways in which positivism treats so-called _objective reality_, the observable world, as unproblematic in theoretical terms. For related issues, see Lapid (1989), Murphy and Tooze (1991a) and J. George (1994). See also Sayer (1992).
2 My reference here is to the 1972 second edition because of Kuhn's useful postscript, which discusses reactions to his ideas, including problems of vagueness of the concept of paradigm itself.
3 This summary rephrases but draws directly on Vasquez's (1983: 18) terms.
4 I have drawn extensively on the work of Michel Foucault for my understanding in this area. See Foucault (1966, 1969, 1971). See also Dillon (1995).
5 See Yosef Lapid's (1989: 239–40) discussion of the post-positivist emphasis on 'an irreducibly three-dimensional space for scientific knowledge'.
6 One of the clearest statements about this has been made by Michel Foucault (1971).
7 Hegemony is a key concept in both neorealist and Gramscian approaches. Indeed, it is useful to focus on this concept and their starkly contrasting approaches to it. I return to this area in chapter 5.
8 On the Bretton Woods system, see, for example, Van der Wee (1987). See also Stubbs and Underhill (1994a).
9 On this point, see also John Ruggie's (1983) arguments concerning 'embedded liberalism'.
10 See also Tooze (1987). 'The present structure of IPE [international political economy] as a field of inquiry is principally the result of two forces and the responses engendered by these forces. The first is the hegemony of the United States which has largely provided the agenda of IPE by defining the central issues and, in a process of intellectual hegemony within the academic study of international relations, the methodology and core concepts for "solving" the problems so defined' (p. 349).
11 Within feminist debates the question of how public/private divides should be addressed as part of efforts to reclaim politics has been a key area of contestation (see, for example, Phillips 1991). In historical context, see Wollstonecraft (1985 (1792)).

12 I am drawing here on Richard Ashley's (1988b) use of presence and absence in considering sovereignty.
13 Doreen Massey's work on gender and changes in the social and spatial organization of capitalist production has been influential in this area (see Massey 1994, 1995).

Chapter 4 Beyond the Normative Divide

1 The two key historical centres of the development of realist approaches have been Britain and the USA with the latter's influence growing significantly after World War Two (see Olson and Groom 1991: 139–40; Hollis and Smith 1991: 20–8). Among realist writings, see in particular Wight (1946, 1978), Waltz (1959) and Bull (1977). See also Justin Rosenberg's (1994) critique of realist theory.
2 See Walker (1993) on the question of theory and 'the politics of forgetting'.
3 One of the interesting aspects of this critical writing outside of this volume's main concerns is a more subtle approach to historical and more recent forms of realism, together with explorations of the partialities of established interpretations of them and alternative possibilities (see especially Ashley 1984; Walker 1993: 26–49; Spegele 1996).
4 It is essential to recognize that they feature contrasting theoretical perspectives (see, for example, Linklater 1990; Frost 1986; Onuf 1989).
5 A useful discussion of this area has been undertaken by Robert Jackson (1995).
6 Martin Wight's work has been influential in this respect. See Wight (1977, 1978, 1991) and Bull and Holbraad (1978) on Wight's 'ambivalent' position with regard to realism.
7 See, in particular, Walker (1988b, 1990) and Ashley and Walker (1990).
8 See also Ashley (1988b, 1989, 1991), Weber (1994) and Bierstecker and Weber (1996). On gendered power in politics, see *Alternatives* (1993).
9 Parts of the following discussion were first presented at international political economy panels of the British International Studies Association and International Studies Association (Youngs 1994). I am grateful for comments from participants and from Roger Tooze and Richard Little. See Jim George's (1994) extensive consideration of Ashley's work.
10 See discussion by Ashley (1980: 9–49) of Choucri and North (1975), particularly the concept of 'lateral pressure'.
11 See Ashley's (1980: 221–4) further examination of interdependence.
12 In this general area, Ashley has noted the work of Jürgen Habermas (see Ashley 1980: 251; see also Ashley 1981; McCarthy 1992; Habermas 1971a, 1971b, 1992).
13 Limited attention has been given here to Ashley's detailed investigation of the 'security problematique' (see especially Ashley 1980: 174–205).
14 See also Frost's (1996) arguments on ethics in the study of international relations.
15 See in this context David Held's (1995) work on the 'tension between the

ideas of the modern state and of democracy'.

16 See Held (1995: 159–88) on 'sites of power'.

17 The critical work of David Campbell (1992, 1993) has also been influential in relation to foreign policy and identity questions. See also Dillon (1989).

18 The collection of essays in Kofman and Youngs (1996a) usefully demonstrates this. See also Castles and Miller (1993), Waever et al. (1993), Held (1993, 1995) and Sassen (1996).

19 John Hoffman's (1995) assessment of 'democracy and the movement beyond the state' is interesting in this respect. See also Rob Walker's (1993: 141–58) discussion of democracy. On the issue of separateness in world politics, Immanuel Kant's late eighteenth-century notion of the potential for 'perpetual peace' among states remains one of the most influential theses: 'Kant aspired to the continuities of universal reason from the perfectible individual to the perfectible species' (Walker 1993: 138). See Kant (1983), Brown (1992), Franke (1995) and MacMillan (1995).

20 A recent assessment of the triad of economies has been made by Agnew and Corbridge (1995: 155–63).

21 James Anderson and James Goodman (1995) have given useful consideration to the EU and globalization in this regard. See also Ruggie (1993).

Chapter 5 States, Time and Space

1 The field of postcolonial studies has provided important perspectives in this area (see Ashcroft, Griffiths and Tiffin 1989; Said 1991, 1994; Bhabha 1994; Darby 1996).

2 With regard to this point and the following section, see the discussion of territoriality and transformation by Ruggie (1993). See also Ruggie (1989).

3 See also Herz (1973), Walker (1993: 135–8) and an examination by Richard Harknett (1996) of current perspectives on Herz's assessment of territorial security. With regard to points in this section as well as the broader preoccupations of this volume, note also Richard Ashley's (1981) assessment of Herz's 'unique' brand of realism.

4 Many of these have already been referred to in earlier chapters. Among the most influential are Keohane (1984, 1986a, 1989) and Gilpin (1987).

5 This mainstream approach to governance, however, is distinct from Foucaultian perspectives on 'governmentality', which will be referred to in the next chapter (see Dillon 1995; Burchell, Gordon and Miller 1991).

6 One of the most extensive considerations of this area remains the collection of essays in Buzan and Jones (1981).

7 Mark Rupert's (1995) detailed assessment of mass production and US global power is notable in this context. See also Robinson (1996) and Gill and Mittelman (1997).

8 See in particular Robert Cox's (1981) distinction between the *pax Britannica* and *pax Americana*. See also Cox (1987), Gill (1993b), Augelli and Murphy (1988) and Gill (1997b).

9 See Björn Hettne's (1995a: 17–19) consideration of alternative scenarios be-

tween 'global interdependence and a fragmented world'.

10 Anthony Giddens's extensive discussion of 'post-traditional' tendencies and their implications for radical politics is influential in this respect (see, for example, Giddens 1991a, 1994). See also Beck (1997) on 'reflexive modernization' and Bauman (1992) on 'postmodernity'.

11 See, for example, the examination of 'glocalization' by Lash and Urry (1994) and Agnew and Corbridge (1995). See also Harvey (1990).

12 My understanding of the importance of the body in addressing social power has been particularly influenced by Foucaultian insights (see, for example, Foucault 1975, 1976, 1984a, 1984b, 1988a, 1990; Martin 1988; see also Youngs forthcoming b).

13 Chang and Ling criticize Gramscian analysis in this context for limited attention to 'the dynamics of local–global interaction'.

14 See Doreen Massey's (1994: 249–72) discussion of 'politics and space/time'.

Chapter 6 Political Economy of Spatiality

1 The following points were presented first in Youngs (1997b). See also Youngs (1997d).

2 See in relation to the following points Robert Boyer's (1996) discussion of 'state and market: a new engagement for the twenty-first century?'

3 This term recalls John Burton's (1972) early work on 'cobweb' models of 'world society'. Burton's arguments and their attention to 'transactions' and 'communications' are worth revisiting in the light of current considerations of processes of globalization.

4 Hirst and Thompson (1996) stress the continuing key role of the state in this respect: 'While the state's capacities for governance have changed and in many respects (especially national macroeconomic management) have weakened considerably, it remains a pivotal institution, especially in terms of creating the conditions for effective international governance' (p. 170).

5 Another concept being mobilized in this respect is 'the post-national state' (Drache 1996).

6 See, for example, McNay (1992) and Balbus (1988) on this point. See also Sawicki (1988) for a discussion of concerns shared by Foucault and feminists.

7 It is important to note that control over the movement of people is increasingly being identified as an area in which state control could be understood as holding strong. See Saskia Sassen's (1996: 59–99) consideration of immigration. See also Hirst and Thompson (1996): 'While the state's exclusive control of territory has been reduced by international markets and new communications media, it still retains one central role that ensures a large measure of territorial control – the regulation of populations. People are less mobile than money, goods or ideas: in a sense they remain "nationalized", dependent on passports, visas, and residence and labour qualifications. The democratic state's role as the possessor of a territory in which it regulates its population gives it a definite legitimacy internationally in a way no other agency could have in that

it can speak for that population' (p. 171). See also Pellerin (1996) on global restructuring and international migration, and Icduygu (1996) on the complexities of immigration and formal citizenship issues.

8 Risk issues have been prominent in assessments of globalization (see Giddens 1991b, 1994; see also Beck 1992, Lash and Urry 1994).

9 Samuel Huntington's (1993: 22) 'clash of civilizations' thesis could also be viewed in this way. He argued that in the new era: 'The great divisions among humankind and the dominating source of conflict will be cultural.' The grand picture that this thesis paints of world politics replaces the ideological contest with one that is cultural, and posits 'Western' with 'non-Western' civilizations as a new form of oppositional analytical framework. Culture replaces ideology as a prime source of conflict, but surprisingly little attention is given to detailed explanation of what is meant by the term culture or what distinguishes it from ideology. 'Common religion and civilizational identity' (p. 29) are located under the cultural heading, with clear references to historically developed commonalities of values and experience. But his discussion of 'Western concepts' such as individualism, liberalism and human rights (pp. 40–1) strays into ideological territory. Huntington's arguments demonstrate that in the future we are likely to need to give much more thought to concepts such as ideology and culture and their meanings and associations.

10 See Petrella (1996) on 'world' investment, production and consumption patterns: 'business culture is said to obey a world strategy even if it is difficult to identify the specific territorial and legal basis of these organizations' (p. 71).

11 Lash and Urry's (pp. 151–6) fuller distinctions between types of city usefully moves towards consideration of the detailed historical differences and developments in the economies of major cities, including in relation to manufacturing and service sectors, and the communications networks and associated qualities that contribute to global city status.

12 See discussion by Carole Pateman (1988: 19–38) of 'traditional' patriarchal emphasis on paternal relations, and 'modern patriarchy' as 'fraternal, contractual'. See also the assessment by Andrée Michel (1995: 38) of 'the dominant patriarchal model which governs North–South exchanges'. For further related analysis, see also Peterson and Runyan (1993), Elson (1995), Momsen and Kinnaird (1993), Marchand and Parpart (1995) and Sylvester (1993).

13 I would therefore disagree with the place that Lash and Urry (p. 311) allocate to this issue in saying towards the close of their study: 'Finally, we should note how the globalization–localization processes analysed here impact very significantly on women.' Points raised in this and earlier chapters referring to the _fundamental_ relevance of gender analysis to the conceptualization of global relations are relevant here.

Bibliography

Agnew, J. and Corbridge, S. 1995: *Mastering Space: hegemony, territory and international political economy.* London: Routledge.

Albrow, M. 1996: *The Global Age: state and society beyond modernity.* Cambridge: Polity.

Alexander, T. 1996: *Unravelling Global Apartheid: an overview of world politics.* Cambridge: Polity.

Alternatives 1993: Special Issue. Feminists Write International Relations. 18(1).

Alternatives 1994: Special Issue. Against Global Apartheid: contemporary perspectives on world order and world order studies. 19(2).

Ambrose, S. E. 1988: *Rise to Globalism: American Foreign Policy Since 1938,* 5th edn. New York: Penguin.

Anderson, J. and Goodman, J. 1995: Regions, states and the European Union: modernist reaction or postmodern adaptation? *Review of International Political Economy,* 2, 600–31.

Arac, J. (ed.) 1988: *After Foucault: humanistic knowledge, postmodern challenges.* New Brunswick, NJ: Rutgers University Press.

Ashcroft, B., Griffiths, G. and Tiffin, H. 1989: *The Empire Writes Back: theory and practice in post-colonial literatures.* London: Routledge.

Ashley, R. K. 1980: *The Political Economy of War and Peace: the Sino-Soviet-American triangle and the modern security problematique.* London: Pinter.

Ashley, R. K. 1981: Political realism and human interests. *International Studies Quarterly,* 25, 204–36.

Ashley, R. K. 1983: Three modes of economism. *International Studies Quarterly,* 27, 463–96.

Ashley, R. K. 1984: The poverty of neorealism. *International Organization,* 38, 225–86.

Ashley, R. K. 1987: The geopolitics of geopolitical space: toward a critical social theory of international politics. *Alternatives,* 12, 403–34.

Ashley, R. K. 1988a: Geopolitics, supplementary, criticism: a reply to Professors Roy and Walker. *Alternatives,* 13, 87–102.

Ashley, R. K. 1988b: Untying the sovereign state: a double reading of the anarchy problematique. *Millennium: Journal of International Studies*, 17, 227–62.

Ashley, R. K. 1989: Living on border lines: man, poststructuralism, and war. In Der Derian and Shapiro, 259–321.

Ashley, R. K. 1991: The state of the discipline: realism under challenge. In Higgott and Richardson, 37–69.

Ashley, R. K. and Walker, R. B. J. 1990: Reading dissidence/writing the discipline: crisis and the question of sovereignty in international studies. *International Studies Quarterly*, 34, 367–416.

Ashworth, G. (ed.) 1995: *A Diplomacy of the Oppressed: new directions in international feminism*. London: Zed.

Augelli, E. and Murphy, C. 1988: *America's Quest for Supremacy and the Third World: a Gramscian analysis*. London: Pinter.

Balbus, I. D. 1988: Disciplining women: Michel Foucault and the power of feminist discourse. In Arac, 138–60.

Baldwin, D. 1993a: Neoliberalism, neorealism and world politics. In Baldwin 1993b, 3–25.

Baldwin, D. (ed.) 1993b: *Neorealism and Neoliberalism: the contemporary debate*. New York: Columbia University Press.

Barnet, R. J. and Cavanagh, J. 1994: *Global Dreams: imperial corporations and the new world order*. New York: Simon and Shuster.

Bauman, Z. 1992: *Intimations of Postmodernity*. London: Routledge.

Beck, U. 1992: *Risk Society: towards a new modernity*. London: Sage.

Beck, U. 1997: *The Reinvention of Politics: rethinking modernity in the global social order*. Cambridge: Polity.

Bernauer, J. W. and Rasmussen, D. (eds) 1988: *The Final Foucault*. Cambridge, Mass.: MIT Press.

Bhabha, H. K. 1994: *The Location of Culture*. London: Routledge.

Biersteker, T. J. and Weber, C. 1996: *State Sovereignty as Social Construct*. Cambridge: Cambridge University Press.

Booth, K. and Smith, S. (eds) 1995: *International Relations Theory Today*. Cambridge: Polity.

Boyer, R. 1996: State and market: a new engagement for the twenty-first century? In Boyer and Drache, 84–114.

Boyer, R. and Drache, D. (eds) 1996: *States Against Markets: the limits of globalization*. London: Routledge.

Brace, L. and Hoffman, J. (eds) 1997: *Reclaiming Sovereignty*. London: Pinter.

Brown, C. 1992: *International Relations Theory: new normative approaches*. Hemel Hempstead: Harvester Wheatsheaf.

Bull, H. 1966: International theory: the case for a classical approach. *World Politics*, 18, 361–77. Also in Knorr and Rosenau, 20–38.

Bull, H. 1977: *The Anarchical Society: a study of order in world politics*. London: Macmillan.

Bull, H. and Holbraad, C. 1978: Intro. in Wight, 9–29.

Burchell, G., Gordon, C. and Miller, P. (eds) 1991: *The Foucault Effect: studies in governmentality*. Hemel Hempstead: Harvester Wheatsheaf.

Burton, J. 1972: *World Society*. Cambridge: Cambridge University Press.

Butler, J. 1990: *Gender Trouble: feminism and the subversion of identity*. New York: Routledge.

Buzan, B. 1991: *People, States and Fear: an agenda for international security studies in the post-cold war era*, 2nd edn. Hemel Hempstead: Harvester Wheatsheaf.

Buzan, B. and Jones, R. J. B. (eds) 1981: *Change in the Study of International Relations: the evaded dimension*. London: Pinter.

Buzan, B., Jones, C. and Little, R. 1993: *The Logic of Anarchy: neorealism to structural realism*. New York: Columbia University Press.

Camilleri, J. A. and Falk, J. 1992: *The End of Sovereignty? The politics of a shrinking and fragmenting world*. Aldershot: Edward Elgar.

Campbell, D. 1992: *Writing Security: United States foreign policy and the politics of identity*. Manchester: Manchester University Press.

Campbell, D. 1993: *Politics Without Principle: sovereignty, ethics, and narratives of the Gulf War*. Boulder, Colo.: Lynne Rienner.

Carr, E. H. 1946: *The Twenty Years' Crisis 1919–1939: an introduction to the study of international relations*, 2nd edn. 1st edn published 1939. London: Macmillan.

Castles, S. and Miller, M. J. 1993: *The Age of Migration: international population movements in the modern world*. Basingstoke: Macmillan.

Cerny, P. G. 1995: Globalization and the changing logic of collective action. *International Organization*, 49, 595–625.

Cerny, P. G. 1996: What next for the state? In Kofman and Youngs 1996a.

Chang, K. and Ling, L. H. M. 1995: Globalization and its intimate other: the Filipina maid community in Hong Kong. Paper presented at Gender and Global Restructuring: Shifting Sites and Sightings Conference, University of Amsterdam, 12–13 May. (Forthcoming in Marchand and Runyan.)

Chomsky, N. 1992: A view from below. In Hogan, 137–50.

Choucri, N. and North, R. C. 1975: *Nations in Conflict: national growth and international violence*. San Francisco, Calif.: W. H. Freeman.

Clark, I. 1997: *Globalization and Fragmentation: international relations in the twentieth century*. Oxford: Oxford University Press.

Cohen, S. B. 1994: Geopolitics in the new world era: a new perspective on an old discipline. In Demko and Wood, 15–48.

Commission on Global Governance 1995: *Our Global Neighbourhood*. Oxford: Oxford University Press.

Cox, R. W. 1981: Social forces, states and world orders: beyond international relations theory. *Millennium: Journal of International Studies*, 10, 127–55.

Cox, R. W. 1987: *Production, Power and World Order: social forces in the making of history*. New York: Columbia University Press.

Cox, R. W. 1994: Global restructuring: making sense of the changing international political economy. In Stubbs and Underhill 1994b, 45–59.

Cox, R. W. 1995: Critical political economy. In Hettne 1995a, 31–45.

Cox, R. W. 1997: *The New Realism: perspectives on multilateralism and world order*. London: Macmillan.

Craib, I. 1992: *Anthony Giddens*. London: Routledge.

Czempiel, E. O. and Rosenau, J. N. 1989: *Global Changes and Theoretical Challenges: approaches to world politics for the 1990s*. Lexington, Mass.: Lexington.

Dalby, S. 1990: _Creating the Second Cold War: the discourse of politics._ London: Pinter.
Dalby, S. 1996: Crossing disciplinary boundaries: political geography and international relations after the cold war. In Kofman and Youngs 1996a.
Darby, P. (ed.) 1997: _At the Edge of International Relations: postcolonialism, gender and dependency._ London: Pinter.
Darby, P. and Paolini, A. J. 1994: Bridging international relations and post-colonialism. _Alternatives,_ 19, 371–97.
Demko, G. J. and Wood, W. B. (eds) 1994: _Reordering the World: geopolitical perspectives on the 21st century._ Boulder, Colo.: Westview.
Der Derian, J. 1991: _On Diplomacy: a genealogy of western estrangement._ Oxford: Blackwell.
Der Derian, J. and Shapiro, M. (eds) 1989: _International/Intertextual Relations: postmodern readings of world politics._ New York: Lexington.
Dicken, P. 1992: _Global Shift,_ 2nd edn. London: Paul Chapman.
Dillon, M. 1989: _The Falklands, Politics and War._ London: Macmillan.
Dillon, M. 1995: Sovereignty and governmentality: from the problematics of the 'new world order' to the ethical problematic of the world order. _Alternatives,_ 20, 323–68.
Di Stefano, C. 1991: _Configurations of Masculinity: a feminist perspective on modern political theory._ Ithaca, NY: Cornell University Press.
Drache, D. 1996: From Keynes to K-Mart: competitiveness in a corporate age. In Boyer and Drache, 31–61.
Drucker, P. F. 1994: _Post-Capitalist Society._ New York: HarperCollins.
Dworkin, A. 1981: _Pornography: men possessing women._ London: Women's Press.
Eisenstein, Z. 1994: _The Colour of Gender: reimagining democracy._ Berkeley, Calif.: University of California Press.
Elson, D. (ed.) 1995: _Male Bias in the Development Process,_ 2nd edn. Manchester: Manchester University Press.
Enloe, C. 1983: _Does Khaki Become You?_ Boston, Mass.: South End Press.
Enloe, C. 1990: _Bananas, Beaches and Bases: making feminist sense of international politics._ Berkeley, Calif.: University of California Press.
Enloe, C. 1993: _The Morning After: sexual politics at the end of the cold war._ Berkeley, Calif.: University of California Press.
Evans, T. 1996: _US Hegemony and the Project of Universal Human Rights._ London: Macmillan.
Featherstone, M. (ed.) 1990: _Global Culture: nationalism, globalization and modernity._ London: Sage.
Featherstone, M., Lash, S. and Robertson, R. (eds) 1995: _Global Modernities._ London: Sage.
Foucault, M. 1961: _Folie et déraison: histoire de la folie à l'âge classique._ Paris: Plon. Tr. by R. Howard as _Madness and Civilization,_ New York: Pantheon, 1965.
Foucault, M. 1963: _Naissance de la clinique: une archéologie du regard médical._ Paris: Presses Universitaires de France (rev. edn. 1972). Tr. by A. Sheridan Smith as _The Birth of the Clinic: an archaeology of medical perception,_ New York: Pantheon, 1973.
Foucault, M. 1966: _Les Mots et les choses,_ Paris: Gallimard. Tr. by A. Sheridan

Smith as *The Order of Things*, London: Tavistock Publications, 1970.

Foucault, M. 1969: *L'Archéologie du savoir*. Paris: Gallimard. Tr. by A. Sheridan Smith as *The Archaeology of Knowledge*, London: Tavistock Publications, 1970.

Foucault, M. 1971: *L'Ordre du discours*. Paris: Gallimard. Tr. by I. McLeod as The Order of Discourse, in M. Shapiro (ed.) 1984: *Language and Politics*, Oxford: Blackwell.

Foucault, M. 1975: *Surveiller et punir: naissance de la prison*. Paris: Gallimard. Tr. by A. Sheridan as *Discipline and Punish: the birth of the prison*, New York: Pantheon, 1977.

Foucault, M. 1976: *Histoire de la sexualité 1: La volonté de savoir*. Tr. as *The History of Sexuality: an introduction*, Harmondsworth: Penguin, 1981.

Foucault, M. 1982: The subject and power. Afterword to H. Dreyfus and P. Rabinow. *Michel Foucault: beyond structuralism and hermeneutics*. Chicago, Ill.: Chicago University Press, 208–26.

Foucault, M. 1984a: *Histoire de la sexualité 2: L'Usage des plaisirs*. Paris: Gallimard. Tr. by R. Hurley as *The Use of Pleasure*, New York: Pantheon, 1985.

Foucault, M. 1984b: *Histoire de la sexualité 3: Le Souci de soi*. Paris: Gallimard. Tr. as *The Care of the Self*, Harmondsworth: Penguin, 1990.

Foucault, M. 1988a: Technologies of the self. In Martin, Gutman and Hutton, 16–49.

Foucault, M. 1988b: The political technology of individuals. In Martin, Gutman and Hutton, 145–62.

Foucault, M. 1990: *Politics, Philosophy, Culture: interviews and other writings 1977–1984*. Ed. with intro. by L. D. Kritzman. Tr. by A. Sheridan and others. New York: Routledge.

Foucault, M. 1991a: Governmentality. In Burchell, Gordon and Miller, 87–104.

Foucault, M. 1991b: Politics and the study of discourse. In Burchell, Gordon and Miller, 53–72.

Foucault, M. 1991c: Questions of method. In Burchell, Gordon and Miller, 73–86.

Franke, M. F. N. 1995: Immanuel Kant and the (im)possibility of international relations theory. *Alternatives*, 20, 279–322.

Friedman, J. 1994: *Cultural Identity and Global Process*. London: Sage.

Frost, M. 1986: *Towards a Normative Theory of International Relations: a critical analysis of the philosophical and methodological assumptions in the discipline with proposals towards a substantive normative theory*. Cambridge: Cambridge University Press.

Frost, M. 1996: *Ethics in International Relations: a constitutive theory*. Cambridge: Cambridge University Press.

Fukuyama, F. 1992: *The End of History and the Last Man*. London: Penguin.

George, J. 1989: International relations and the search for thinking space: another view of the third debate. *International Studies Quarterly*, 33, 269–79.

George, J. 1994: *Discourses of Global Politics: a critical (re)introduction to international relations*. Boulder, Colo.: Lynne Rienner.

George, J. and Campbell, D. 1990: Patterns of dissent and the celebration of difference: critical social theory and international relations. *International Studies*

Quarterly, 34, 269–93.

George, S. 1986: _How the Other Half Dies: the real reasons for world hunger_. London: Penguin.

George, S. 1989: _A Fate Worse Than Debt_. London: Penguin.

Gibson-Graham, J. K. 1996: _The End of Capitalism (As We Knew It): a feminist critique of political economy_. Oxford: Blackwell.

Giddens, A. 1979: _Central Problems in Social Theory_. Berkeley, Calif.: University of California Press.

Giddens, A. 1984: _The Constitution of Society: Outline of a Theory of Structuration_. Cambridge: Polity.

Giddens, A. 1987: _Social Theory and Modern Sociology_. Cambridge: Polity.

Giddens, A. 1991a: _Modernity and Self Identity: Self and Society in the Late Modern Age_. Cambridge: Polity.

Giddens, A. 1991b: _The Consequences of Modernity_. Cambridge: Polity.

Giddens, A. 1994: _Beyond Left and Right: The Future of Radical Politics_. Cambridge: Polity.

Gill, S. 1991: Historical materialism, Gramsci, and international political economy. In Murphy and Tooze 1991b, 51–75.

Gill, S. 1993a: Gramsci and global politics: towards a post-hegemonic research agenda. In Gill 1993b, 1–18.

Gill, S. (ed.) 1993b: _Gramsci, Historical Materialism and International Relations_. Cambridge: Cambridge University Press.

Gill, S. 1994: Knowledge, politics and neo-liberal political economy. In Stubbs and Underhill 1994b, 75–88.

Gill, S. 1995: Theorizing the interregnum: the double movement and global politics in the 1990s. In Hettne 1995a, 65–99.

Gill, S. (ed.) 1997a: _Globalization, Democratization and Multilateralism_. London: Macmillan.

Gill, S. 1997b: Transformation and innovation in the study of world order. In Gill and Mittelman.

Gill, S. and Law, D. 1988: _The Global Political Economy: perspectives, problems and policies_. Hemel Hempstead: Harvester Wheatsheaf.

Gill, S. and Mittelman, J. H. (ed.) 1997: _Innovation and Transformation in International Studies_. Cambridge: Cambridge University Press.

Gilpin, R. 1972: The politics of transnational economic relations. In Keohane and Nye, 48–69.

Gilpin, R. 1975: _Power and the Multinational Corporation_. New York: Basic Books.

Gilpin, R. 1981: _War and Change in World Politics_. New York: Cambridge University Press.

Gilpin, R. with the assistance of Gilpin, J. M. 1987: _The Political Economy of International Relations_. Princeton, NJ: Princeton University Press.

Gordon, C. 1991: Governmental rationality: an introduction. In Burchell, Gordon and Miller, 1–51.

Grant, R. and Newland, K. (eds) 1991: _Gender and International Relations_. Milton Keynes: Open University Press.

Habermas, J. 1971a: _Legitimation Crisis_. Boston, Mass: Beacon Press.

Habermas, J. 1971b: *Toward a Rational Society*. Boston, Mass: Beacon Press.

Habermas, J. 1992: *Moral Consciousness and Communicative Action*. Cambridge: Polity.

Halliday, F. 1995: The end of the cold war and international relations: some analytic and theoretical conclusions. In Booth and Smith, 38–61.

Harcourt, W. (ed.) 1994: *Feminist Perspectives on Sustainable Development*. London: Zed (in association with Society for International Development).

Harcourt, W. (ed.) Forthcoming: *Women@Internet*. London: Zed.

Harding, S. 1991: *Whose Science? Whose Knowledge?* Ithaca, NY: Cornell University Press.

Harknett, R. J. 1996: Territoriality in the nuclear era. In Kofman and Youngs 1996a.

Harris, N. 1990: *The End of the Third World: newly industrializing countries and the decline of an ideology*. London: Penguin.

Harvey, D. 1990: *The Condition of Postmodernity: an enquiry into the origins of cultural change*. Oxford: Blackwell.

Held, D. 1991a: Democracy, the nation-state and the global system. In Held 1991b, 197–235.

Held, D. (ed.) 1991b: *Political Theory Today*. Stanford, Calif.: Stanford University Press.

Held, D. (ed.) 1993: *Prospects for Democracy: north, south, east, west*. Cambridge: Polity.

Held, D. 1995: *Democracy and the Global Order: from modern state to cosmopolitan governance*. Cambridge: Polity.

Hennessy, R. 1993: *Materialist Feminism and the Politics of Discourse*. London: Routledge.

Henrikson, A. K. 1994: The power and politics of maps. In Demko and Wood, 49–70.

Herz, J. H. 1957: Rise and demise of the territorial state. *World Politics*, IX, 473–93.

Herz, J. H. 1968: The territorial state revisited: reflections on the future of the nation-state. *Polity*, 1, 11–34.

Herz, J. H. 1973: *The Nation-State and the Crisis of World Politics*. New York: David McKay.

Hettne, B. (ed.) 1995a: *International Political Economy: understanding global disorder*. London: Zed.

Hettne, B. 1995b: Introduction: the international political economy of transformation. In Hettne 1995a, 1–30.

Higgott, R. and Richardson, J. L. (eds) 1991: *International Relations: global and Australian perspectives on an evolving discipline*. Canberra: Australian National University.

Hill, C. and Beshoff, P. (eds) 1994: *Two Worlds of International Relations: academics and practitioners and the trade in ideas*. London: Routledge.

Hindess, B. 1996: *Discourses of Power: from Hobbes to Foucault*. Oxford: Blackwell.

Hirst, P. 1997: *From Statism to Pluralism*. London: University College London.

Hirst, P. and Thompson, G. 1996: *Globalization in Question: the international economy and the possibilities of governance*. Cambridge: Polity.

Hobbes, T. 1968 (first published 1651): *Leviathan*. Ed. with intro. by C. B. Macpherson. Harmondsworth: Penguin.

Hoekman, B. M. and Kostecki, M. M. 1995: *The Political Economy of the World Trading System: from GATT to WTO*. Oxford: Oxford University Press.

Hoffman, J. 1995: *Beyond the State: an introductory critique*. Cambridge: Polity.

Hoffman, M. 1987: Critical theory and the inter-paradigm debate. *Millennium: Journal of International Studies*, 16, 231–49.

Hogan, M. J. (ed.) 1992: *The End of the Cold War: its meanings and implications*. Cambridge: Cambridge University Press.

Hollis, M. and Smith, S. 1991: *Explaining and Understanding International Relations*. Oxford: Clarendon Press.

Holm, H. H. and Sørensen, G. (eds) 1995: *Whose World Order? Uneven globalization and the end of the cold war*. Boulder, Colo.: Westview.

Holsti, K. J. 1985: *The Dividing Discipline*. Winchester, Mass.: Allen and Unwin.

Huntington, S. P. 1993: The clash of civilizations? *Foreign Affairs*, 72(3), 22–49.

Icduygu, A. 1996: Citizenship at a crossroads: immigration and nation-state. In Kofman and Youngs 1996a, 150–620.

Jackson, R. H. 1993: *Quasi-States: sovereignty, international relations and the Third World*. Cambridge: Cambridge University Press.

Jackson, R. H. 1995: The political theory of international society. In Booth and Smith, 110–28.

Jameson, F. 1991: *Postmodernism, or, the Cultural Logic of Late Capitalism*. London: Verso.

Johnston, D. 1991: Constructing the periphery in modern global politics. In Murphy and Tooze 1991b, 149–70.

Jones, R. J. B. 1995: *Globalisation and Interdependence in the International Political Economy: rhetoric and reality*. London: Pinter.

Jones, R. J. B. and Willetts, P. (eds) 1984: *Interdependence on Trial*. London: Pinter.

Journal of International Affairs. 1997: Special Issue: Privatization: Political and Economic Challenges, 50(2).

Kant, I. 1983: *Perpetual Peace and Other Essays*. Tr. by T. Humphrey. Indianapolis, Ind.: Hackett Publishing.

Kaplan, M. 1957: *System and Process in International Politics*. New York: Wiley.

Kaplan, M. 1966: The new great debate: traditionalism vs science in international relations. *World Politics*, 19, 2–20. Also in Knorr and Rosenau, 39–61.

Keat, R. and Urry, J. 1982: *Social Theory as Science*, 2nd edn. London: Routledge and Kegan Paul.

Kennedy, P. 1989: *The Rise and Fall of the Great Powers: economic change and military conflict from 1500–2000*. London: Fontana.

Kennedy, P. 1994: *Preparing for the Twenty-First Century*. London: Fontana.

Keohane, R. O. 1984: *After Hegemony: cooperation and discord in the world political economy*. Princeton, NJ: Princeton University Press.

Keohane, R. O. (ed.) 1986a: *Neorealism and its Critics*. New York: Columbia University Press.

Keohane, R. O. 1986b: Theory of world politics: structural realism and beyond.

In Keohane 1986a, 158–203.

Keohane, R. O. 1989: *International Institutions and State Power*. Boulder, Colo.: Westview.

Keohane, R. O. 1993: Institutional theory and the realist challenge after the cold war. In Baldwin 1993b, 269–300.

Keohane, R. O. and Nye, J. S. (eds) 1972: *Transnational Relations and World Politics*. Cambridge, Mass.: Harvard University Press.

Keohane, R. O. and Nye, J. S. 1989 (first published 1977): *Power and Interdependence: world politics in transition*, 2nd edn. Boston, Mass.: Little, Brown.

King, A. D. 1995: The times and spaces of modernity (or who needs postmodernism?). In Featherstone, Lash and Robertson, 108–23.

Knorr, K. and Rosenau, J. N. (eds) 1969: *Contending Approaches to International Politics*. Princeton, NJ: Princeton University Press.

Knox, P. L. and Taylor, P. J. (eds) 1995: *World Cities in a World-System*. Cambridge: Cambridge University Press.

Kobayashi, A. 1994a: For the sake of the children: Japanese/Canadian workers/mothers. In Kobayashi 1994b, 45–72.

Kobayashi, A. (ed.) 1994b: *Women, Work, and Place*. Montreal: McGill-Queen's University Press.

Kobayashi, A., Peake, L., Benenson, H. and Pickles, K. 1994: Introduction: placing women and work. In Kobayashi 1994b, xi–xlv.

Kofman, E. and Youngs, G. (eds) 1996a: *Globalization: theory and practice*. London: Pinter.

Kofman, E. and Youngs, G. 1996b: Intro. In Kofman and Youngs 1996a.

Krasner, S. D. (ed.) 1983: *International Regimes*. Ithaca NY: Cornell University Press.

Krause, J. 1996: Gender inequalities and feminist politics in global perspective. In Kofman and Youngs 1996a.

Kuhn, T. S. 1972: *The Structure of Scientific Revolution*, 2nd edn. Chicago, Ill.: Chicago University Press.

Lapid, J. 1989: The third debate: on the prospects of international theory in a post-positivist era. *International Studies Quarterly*, 33, 235–54.

Lash, S. and Urry, J. 1994: *Economies of Signs and Space*. London: Sage.

Lash, S., Szerszynski, B. and Wynne, B. (eds) 1996: *Risk, Environment and Modernity*. London: Sage.

Leung, B. 1995: Women and social change: the impact of industrialization on women in Hong Kong. In Pearson and Leung, 1995b, 22–46.

Linklater, A. 1990: *Men and Citizens in the Theory of International Relations*. Basingstoke: Macmillan.

Little, R. 1995: International relations and the triumph of capitalism. In Booth and Smith, 62–89.

McCarthy, T. 1992: Intro. In Habermas 1992, vii–xiii.

McGrew, A. G., Lewis, P. G. et al. 1992: *Global Politics: globalization and the nation-state*. Cambridge: Polity.

Maclean, J. 1981: Political theory, international theory and problems of ideology. *Millennium: Journal of International Studies*, 10, 102–25.

Maclean, J. 1984: Interdependence – an ideological intervention in international relations? In Jones and Willetts, 130–66.

Maclean, J. 1988: Marxism and international relations: a strange case of mutual neglect. *Millennium: Journal of International Studies*, 17, 295–319.

MacMillan, J. 1995: A Kantian protest against the peculiar discourse of inter-liberal state peace. *Millennium: Journal of International Studies*, 24, 549–62.

McNay, L. 1992: *Foucault and Feminism*. Cambridge: Polity.

Mann, M. 1986: *The Sources of Social Power Vol. 1: A History of Power from the Beginning to AD 1760*. Cambridge: Cambridge University Press.

Mann, M. 1993: *The Sources of Social Power Vol. 2: Rise of Classes and Nation-States*. Cambridge: Cambridge University Press.

Marchand, M. H. 1994: The political economy of north–south relations. In Stubbs and Underhill 1994b, 289–301.

Marchand, M. H. and Parpart, J. L. (eds) 1995: *Feminism/Postmodernism/Development*. London: Routledge.

Marchand, M. H. and Runyan, A. S. (eds) forthcoming: *Gender and Global Restructuring*.

Martin, L. H., Gutman, H. and Hutton, P. H. (eds) 1988: *Technologies of the Self: a seminar with Michel Foucault*. London: Tavistock Publications.

Martin, R. 1988: Truth, power, self: an interview with Michel Foucault, 25 October 1982. In Martin, Gutman and Hutton, 9–15.

Massey, D. 1994: *Space, Place and Gender*. Cambridge: Polity.

Massey, D. 1995: *Spatial Divisions of Labour: social structures and the geography of production*, 2nd edn. London: Macmillan.

Michel, A. 1995: Militarisation of contemporary societies and feminism in the north. In Ashworth, 33–51.

Mies, M. 1986: *Patriarchy and Accumulation on a World Scale: women in the international division of labour*. London: Zed.

Millett, K. 1977: *Sexual Politics*. London: Virago.

Mohammadi, A. (ed.) 1997: *International Communication and Globalization*. London: Sage.

Momsen, J. H. and Kinnaird, V. (eds) 1993: *Different Places, Different Voices: gender and development in Africa, Asia and Latin America*. London: Routledge.

Morgenthau, H. J. and Thompson, K. W. 1985: *Politics Among Nations: the struggle for power and peace*, 6th edn. New York: Knopf (1st edn by Morgenthau published in 1948).

Murphy, C. N. and Tooze, R. 1991a: Getting beyond the 'common sense' of the IPE orthodoxy. In Murphy and Tooze 1991b, 11–31.

Murphy, C. N. and Tooze, R. (eds) 1991b: *The New International Political Economy*. Boulder, Colo.: Lynne Rienner.

Ng, C. H. 1995: Bringing women back in: family change in Hong Kong. In Pearson and Leung 1995b, 74–100.

Nye, J. S. and Keohane, R. O. 1972: Transnational relations and world politics: an introduction. In Keohane and Nye, ix–xxix.

Ohmae, K. 1991: *The Borderless World*. London: HarperCollins.

Okin, S. M. 1991: Gender, the public and private. In Held 1991b, 67–90.

Olson, W. C. and Groom, A. J. R. 1991: *International Relations Then and Now: origins and trends in interpretation*. London: HarperCollins Academic.

Onuf, N. G. 1989: *World of Our Making: rules and rule in social theory and international relations*. Columbia, SC: University of South Carolina Press.

Palan, R. P. and Gills, B. (eds) 1994: *Transcending the State–Global Divide: a neostructuralist agenda in international relations*. Boulder, Colo.: Lynne Rienner.

Paolini, A. 1997: Globalization. In Darby, 33–60.

Parker, G. 1996: Globalization and geopolitical world orders. In Kofman and Youngs 1996a.

Pateman, C. 1988: *The Sexual Contract*. Cambridge: Polity.

Pearson, V. and Leung, B. 1995a: Introduction: perspectives on women's issues in Hong Kong. In Pearson and Leung 1995b, 1–21.

Pearson, V. and Leung, B. (eds) 1995b: *Women in Hong Kong*. Hong Kong: Oxford University Press.

Pearson, V. and Yu, R. Y. M. 1995: Business and pleasure: aspects of the commercial sex industry. In Pearson and Leung 1995b, 244–75.

Pellerin, H. 1996: Global restructuring and international migration: consequences for the globalization of politics. In Kofman and Youngs 1996a, 81–96.

Peterson, V. S. (ed.) 1992a: *Gendered States: (re)visions of international relations theory*. Boulder, Colo.: Lynne Rienner.

Peterson, V. S. 1992b: Transgressing boundaries: theories of knowledge, gender, and international relations. *Millennium: Journal of International Studies*, 21, 183–206.

Peterson, V. S. 1995: Reframing the politics of identity: democracy, globalization and gender. *Political Expressions* 1(1), 1–16.

Peterson, V. S. 1996: Shifting ground(s): epistemological and territorial remapping in the context of globalization(s). In Kofman and Youngs 1996a, 11–28.

Peterson, V. S. and Runyan, A. S. 1993: *Global Gender Issues*. Boulder, Colo.: Westview.

Petrella, R. 1996: Globalization and internationalization: the dynamics of the emerging world order. In Boyer and Drache, 62–83.

Pettman, J. J. 1996a: An international political economy of sex? In Kofman and Youngs 1996a.

Pettman, J. J. 1996b: *Worlding Women: a feminist international politics*. London: Routledge.

Phillips, A. 1991: *Engendering Democracy*. Cambridge: Polity.

Powell, R. 1994: Anarchy in international relations theory: the neorealist–neoliberal debate. *International Organization*, 48, 313–44.

Robertson, R. 1992: *Globalization: social theory and global culture*. London: Sage.

Robinson, W. I. 1996: *Promoting Polyarchy: globalization, US intervention, and hegemony*. Cambridge: Cambridge University Press.

Rose, N. 1996: The death of the social? Re-figuring the territory of government. *Economy and Society*, 25.

Rosenau, J. N. 1990: *Turbulence in World Politics: a theory of change and continuity*. Hemel Hempstead: Harvester Wheatsheaf.

Rosenau, J. N. 1992: Governance, order, and change in world politics. In Rosenau and Czempiel, 1–29.

Rosenau, J. N. and Czempiel, E. O. (eds) 1992: *Governance Without Government: order and change in world politics*. Cambridge: Cambridge University Press.

Rosenau, P. M. 1992: *Post-Modernism and the Social Sciences*. Princeton, NJ: Princeton University Press.

Rosenberg, J. 1994: *The Empire of Civil Society: a critique of the realist theory of international relations*. London: Verso.

Rosow, S. J., Inayatullah, N. and Rupert, M. (eds) 1994: *The Global Economy of Political Space*. Boulder, Colo.: Lynne Rienner.

Ruggie, J. G. 1983: International regimes, transactions, and change: embedded liberalism in the postwar economic order. In Krasner, 195–231.

Ruggie, J. G. 1989: International structure and international transformation: space, time, and method. In Czempiel and Rosenau, 21–36.

Ruggie, J. G. 1993: Territoriality and beyond: problematizing modernity in international relations. *International Organization*, 47, 139–74.

Runyan, A. S. 1996: The places of women in trading places: gendered global/regional regimes and inter-nationalized feminist resistance. In Kofman and Youngs 1996a.

Rupert, M. 1995: *Producing Hegemony: the politics of mass production and American global power*. Cambridge: Cambridge University Press.

Said, E. W. 1991 (first published 1978): *Orientalism: western conceptions of the Orient*. London: Penguin.

Said, E. W. 1994: *Culture and Imperialism*. London: Vintage.

Sassen, S. 1991: *The Global City: New York, London, Tokyo*. Princeton, NJ: Princeton University Press.

Sassen, S. 1996: *Losing Control? Sovereignty in an age of globalization*. New York: Columbia University Press.

Sawicki, J. 1988: Feminism and the power of Foucaldian discourse. In Arac, 161–78.

Sayer, A. 1992: *Method in Social Science: a realist approach*, 2nd edn. London: Routledge.

Scholte, J. A. 1993: *International Relations as Social Change*. Buckingham: Open University Press.

Scholte, J. A. 1996: Beyond the buzzword: towards a critical theory of globalization. In Kofman and Youngs 1996a.

Scott, A. M. 1962: *The Revolution in Statecraft*. Durham, NC: Duke University Press.

Seagrave, S. 1995: *Lords of the Rim: the invisible empire of the overseas Chinese*. London: Bantam.

Shapiro, M. 1989: Textualisimg global politics. In Der Derian and Shapiro, 11–22.

Shapiro, M. and Neaubauer, D. 1990: Spatiality and policy discourse: reading the global city. In Walker and Mendlovitz, 97–124.

Sharoni, S. 1995: *Gender and the Israeli–Palestinian Conflict: the politics of women's resistance*. Syracuse, NY: Syracuse University Press.

Singer, J. D. 1961: The level-of-analysis problem in international relations. In

K. Knorr and S. Verba (eds), *The International System: theoretical essays*. Princeton, NJ: Princeton University Press, 77–92.

Sittirak, S. 1996: *Daughters of Development: the stories of women and the changing environment in Thailand*. Bangkok: Women and Environment Research Network in Thailand.

Skocpol, T. 1979: *States and Social Revolutions: a comparative analysis of France, Russia and China*. Cambridge: Cambridge University Press.

Slater, D. 1996: Other contexts of the global: for a critical geopolitics of north–south relations. In Kofman and Youngs 1996a.

Smith, S. 1995: The self-images of a discipline: a genealogy of international relations theory. In Booth and Smith, 1–37.

Spain, D. 1992: *Gendered Spaces*. London: University of North Carolina Press.

Spegele, R. D. 1992: Richard Ashley's discourse for international relations. *Millennium: Journal of International Studies*, 21, 147–82.

Spegele, R. D. 1996: *Political Realism in International Theory*. Cambridge: Cambridge University Press.

Stopford, J. and Strange, S. 1991: *Rival States, Rival Firms: competition for world market shares*. Cambridge: Cambridge University Press.

Strange, S. (ed.) 1984: *Paths to International Political Economy*. London: George Allen and Unwin.

Strange, S. 1991: An eclectic approach. In Murphy and Tooze 1991b, 33–49.

Strange, S. 1994a: Rethinking structural change in the international political economy: states, firms, and diplomacy. In Stubbs and Underhill 1994b, 103–15.

Strange, S. 1994b: *States and Markets*, 2nd edn. London: Pinter.

Strange, S. 1996: *The Retreat of the State: the diffusion of power in the world economy*. Cambridge: Cambridge University Press.

Stubbs, R. and Underhill, G. R. D. 1994a: Global issues in historical perspective. In Stubbs and Underhill 1994b, 145–75.

Stubbs, R. and Underhill, G. R. D. (eds) 1994b: *Political Economy and the Changing Global Order*. Basingstoke: Macmillan.

Sylvester, C. 1994: *Feminist Theory and International Relations in a Postmodern Era*. Cambridge: Cambridge University Press.

Talalay, M., Farrands, C. and Tooze, R. (eds) 1997: *Technology, Culture and Competitiveness and the World Political Economy*. London: Routledge.

Taylor, P. J. 1994: The state as container: territoriality in the modern world-system. *Progress in Human Geography*, 18, 151–62.

Tickner, J. A. 1991: On the fringes of the world economy: a feminist perspective. In Murphy and Tooze 1991b, 191–206).

Tickner, J. A. 1992: *Gender in International Relations: feminist perspectives on achieving global security*. New York: Columbia University Press.

Tomlinson, J. 1991: *Cultural Imperialism*. London: Pinter.

Tooze, R. 1984: Perspectives and theory: a consumer's guide. In Strange, 1–22.

Tooze, R. 1987: International political economy and international relations: from 'enfant terrible' to child prodigy, or just a cuckoo in the nest? *Millennium: Journal of International Studies*, 16, 349–51.

Tooze, R. 1988: The unwritten preface: 'international political economy' and epistemology. _Millennium: Journal of International Studies_, 17, 285–93.

Tooze, R. 1991: International political economy: An Interim Assessment. In Higgott and Richardson, 191–208.

Tooze, R. 1992: Conceptualizing the global economy. In McGrew, Lewis et al., 233–49.

Tsang, G. Y. 1995: The women's movement at the crossroads. In Pearson and Leung 1995b, 276–91.

Turner, T. E. with Ferguson, B. 1993: _Arise Ye Mighty People! Gender, class and race in popular struggles_. Trenton, NJ: Africa World Press.

Tussie, D. 1987: _The Less Developed Countries and the World Trading System: a challenge to the GATT_. London: Pinter.

UNCTAD (United Nations Conference on Trade and Development) 1996: _World Investment Report: investment, trade and international policy arrangements_. New York: United Nations.

UNDP (United Nations Development Programme) 1996: _Human Development Report 1996_. New York: Oxford University Press.

UNDP (United Nations Development Programme) 1997: _Human Development Report 1997_. New York: Oxford University Press.

Van der Wee, H. 1987: _Prosperity and Upheaval: the world economy 1945–1980_. Harmondsworth: Penguin.

Vasquez, J. A. 1983: _The Power of Power Politics: a critique_. London: Pinter.

Vatikiotis, M. R. J. 1996: _Political Change in Southeast Asia: trimming the banyan tree_. London: Routledge.

Vincent, J. 1981: The Hobbesian tradition in twentieth century international thought. _Millennium: Journal of International Studies_, 10, 91–101.

Vincent, J. 1988: Hedley Bull and order in international politics. _Millennium: Journal of International Studies_, 17, 195–213.

Waever, O., Buzan, B., Kelstrup, M. and Lemaitre, P. 1993: _Identity, Migration and the New Security Agenda in Europe_. London: Pinter.

Walby, S. 1990: _Theorizing Patriarchy_. Oxford: Blackwell.

Walker, R. B. J. 1988a: Genealogy, geopolitics and political community: Richard K. Ashley and the critical social theory of international politics. _Alternatives_, 13, 84–102.

Walker, R. B. J. 1988b: _One World, Many Worlds: struggles for a just world peace_. Boulder, Colo.: Lynne Rienner.

Walker, R. B. J. 1990: Sovereignty, identity, community: reflections on the horizons of contemporary political practice. In Walker and Mendlovitz, 159–85.

Walker, R. B. J. 1993: _Inside/Outside: international relations as political theory_. Cambridge: Cambridge University Press.

Walker, R. B. J. and Mendlovitz, S. H. (eds) 1990: _Contending Sovereignties: redefining political community_. Boulder, Colo.: Lynne Rienner.

Wallerstein, I. 1991: _Unthinking Social Science_. Cambridge: Polity.

Waltz, K. N. 1959: _Man, the State, and War: a theoretical analysis_. New York: Columbia University Press.

Waltz, K. N. 1979: _Theory of International Politics_. New York: McGraw-Hill.

Waltz, K. N. 1986: Reflections on *Theory of International Politics:* a response to my critics. In Keohane 1986a, 322–45.

Weber, C. 1994: *Simulating Sovereignty: intervention, the state, and symbolic exchange.* Cambridge: Cambridge University Press.

Weedon, C. 1987: *Feminist Practice and Poststructuralist Theory.* Oxford: Blackwell.

Wendt, A. E. 1987: The agent-structure problem in international relations theory. *International Organization,* 41, 335–70.

Whitworth, S. 1989: Gender in the inter-paradigm debate. *Millennium: Journal of International Studies,* 18, 265–72.

Whitworth, S. 1994a: *Feminism and International Relations: towards a political economy of gender in interstate and non-governmental institutions.* London: Macmillan.

Whitworth, S. 1994b: Theory as exclusion: gender and international political economy. In Stubbs and Underhill 1994b, 116–29.

Wight, M. 1946: *Power Politics, Looking Forward Pamphlet 8.* London: Royal Insitutute of International Affairs.

Wight, M. 1977: *Systems of States.* Ed. with intro. by H. Bull. Leicester: Leicester University Press.

Wight, M. 1978: *Power Politics.* Ed. by H. Bull and C. Holbraad. Leicester: Leicester University Press.

Wight, M. 1991: *International Theory: the three traditions.* Ed. by G. Wight and B. Porter with intro. by H. Bull. Leicester: Leicester University Press.

Williams, M. 1984: The Third World and global reform. *Review of International Studies,* 10, 79–84.

Williams, M. 1994: *International Economic Organisations and the Third World.* Hemel Hempstead: Harvester Wheatsheaf.

Wollstonecraft, M. 1985 (first published 1792): *Vindication of the Rights of Woman.* Ed. with intro. by M. B. Kramnick. Harmondsworth: Penguin.

Wong, T. W. P. 1995: Women and work: opportunities and experiences. In Pearson and Leung 1995b, 47–73.

World Bank 1997: *World Development Report: the state in a changing world.* Oxford: Oxford University Press.

Young, R. 1990: *White mythologies: writing history and the west.* London: Routledge.

Youngs, G. 1990: An analysis of structural concepts of power in international relations. Unpublished MA thesis, University of Sussex.

Youngs, G. 1994: The knowledge problematic: Richard Ashley and political economy. Paper presented at International Studies Association 35th Annual Convention, Washington, 28 March–1 April. Earlier draft presented at the British International Studies Association Annual Conference, University of Warwick, UK, 14–16 December 1993.

Youngs, G. 1995a: Breaking patriarchal bonds: theorising the global – demythologising the public/private. Paper presented at Gender and Global Restructuring: Shifting Sites and Sightings Conference, University of Amsterdam, 12–13 May.

Youngs, G. 1995b: The body and global political economy: some Foucaultian thoughts. Paper presented at Second Pan-European Conference in International Relations, Fondation nationale des sciences politiques, Paris, 13–16 September.

Youngs, G. 1996a: Dangers of discourse: the case of globalization. In Kofman and Youngs 1996a.

Youngs, G. 1996b: Moving beyond the 'inside/outside' divide. In J. Krause and N. Renwick (eds), _Identities in International Relations_. London: Macmillan.

Youngs, G. 1997a: Culture and the technological imperative: missing dimensions. In Talalay, Farrands and Tooze.

Youngs, G. 1997b: Globalized lives, bounded identities: rethinking inequality in transnational contexts. _Development_, 40(3), 15–21.

Youngs, G. 1997c: Political economy, sovereignty and borders in global contexts. In Brace and Hoffman, 117–33.

Youngs, G. 1997d: Tyranny of distance: reflections on economy and democracy. _Development_, 40(4), 15–19.

Youngs, G. 1998: Timeframes and spatial contexts: understanding democracy and the political ecomony of transition in Hong Kong. _Global Society_ 12(2), 237–49.

Youngs, G. forthcoming a: Breaking patriarchal bonds: demythologizing the public/private. In Marchand and Runyan.

Youngs, G. (ed.) forthcoming b: _Political Economy, Power and the Body: global perspectives_. London: Macmillan.

Youngs, G. forthcoming c: Virtual voices: real lives. In Harcourt.

Zalewski, M. and Parpart, J. L. (eds) 1998: _The 'Man' Question in International Relations_. Boulder, Colo.: Westview.

Zukin, S. 1995: _The Cultures of Cities_. Oxford: Blackwell.

Index